Indian Ethos and Values

FOR LEADERSHIP EXCELLENCE

Indian Ethos and Values

FOR LEADERSHIP EXCELLENCE

K. Nagarajan
Assistant General Manager
The Tamilnadu Industrial Investment Corporation Limited

PUBLISHING FOR ONE WORLD
NEW AGE INTERNATIONAL (P) LIMITED, PUBLISHERS
New Delhi • Bangalore • Chennai • Cochin • Guwahati • Hyderabad
Jalandhar • Kolkata • Lucknow • Mumbai • Ranchi
Visit us at **www.newagepublishers.com**

Published by New Age International (P) Ltd., Publishers
First Edition: 2011

Branches:

- 37/10, 8th Cross (Near Hanuman Temple), Azad Nagar, Chamarajpet, **Bangalore**-560 018. Tel.: (080) 26756823, Telefax: 26756820, E-mail: bangalore@newagepublishers.com
- 26, Damodaran Street, T. Nagar, **Chennai**-600 017. Tel.: (044) 24353401, Telefax: 24351463, E-mail: chennai@newagepublishers.com
- CC-39/1016, Carrier Station Road, Ernakulam South, **Cochin**-682 016. Tel.: (0484) 2377004, Telefax: 4051303, E-mail: cochin@newagepublishers.com
- Hemsen Complex, Mohd. Shah Road, Paltan Bazar, Near Starline Hotel, **Guwahati**-781 008. Tel.: (0361) 2513881, Telefax: 2543669, E-mail: guwahati@newagepublishers.com
- 105, 1st Floor, Madhiray Kaveri Tower, 3-2-19, Azam Jahi Road, Nimboliadda, **Hyderabad**-500 027. Tel.: (040) 24652456, Telefax: 24652457, E-mail:hyderabad@newagepublishers.com
- RDB Chambers (Formerly Lotus Cinema)106A, 1st Floor, S.N. Banerjee Road, **Kolkata**-700 014, Tel.: (033) 22273773, Telefax: 22275247, E-mail:kolkata@newagepublishers.com
- 16-A, Jopling Road, **Lucknow**-226 001. Tel.: (0522) 2209578, 4045297, Telefax: 2204098, E-mail: lucknow@newagepublishers.com
- 142C, Victor House, Ground Floor, N.M. Joshi Marg, Lower Parel, **Mumbai**-400 013, Tel.: (022) 24927869, Telefax: 24915415, E-mail: mumbai@newagepublishers.com
- 22, Golden House, Daryaganj, **New Delhi**-110 002. Tel.: (011) 23262370, 23262368, Telefax: 43551305, E-mail: sales@newagepublishers.com

---

ISBN: 978-81-224-3191-9

₹ 150.00

C-11-01-5289

Printed in India at Glorious Printers, Delhi.
Typeset at Inhouse

PUBLISHING FOR ONE WORLD
NEW AGE INTERNATIONAL (P) LIMITED, PUBLISHERS
4835/24, Ansari Road, Daryaganj, New Delhi-110002
Visit us at **www.newagepublishers.com**

Dedicated
to my Friends
who have already left the world
but made me realize
the futility of
materialistic life

India Preserves the knowledge that preserves the world

—Sri Aurobindo

Preface

Man, as a biological being, is one of the greatest wonders. Every day, millions of human beings take birth into this wonderful world and millions depart from the world, not knowing for sure where they came from and where they go. During their life span, as any biological being, man strives to live a comfortable life, within the boundaries of many constraints that surround him. Any concept that man develops, any tool that man devises, any ideology that man forms, any philosophy that man conceives of will survive the test of time provided they are conducive to human welfare in the sense that they offer him both physical as well as mental comfort. Physical comfort is tangible and it can be measured in terms of material benefits that accrue to man. Mental comfort is one that is difficult to assess and can not be quantified. Hence, human welfare remains a highly elusive concept to define.

Management, as an art and science of getting things done for making effective use of the available resources for the betterment of human society has existed from time immemorial, as a natural process of evolution of human mind. Management, as it obtains today, gives priority, only to add to the material progress which has been taken as the index of growth, development and prosperity. This has reduced the relevance of human values to insignificance. If man goes on to create more and more of material comforts with a view to improving his living conditions, forgetting on the other hand, the need for developing a healthy mind that is the foundation for leading a happy and contented life, he surely misses the greatest opportunity given to him. The advancements in the sphere of science and technology, though have added to the material comforts of man, have grossly failed to make him lead a contented life. Then, there must be something wrong in our understanding as to what a better life is. If one is asked to choose between a materially rich life which lacks mental satisfaction and a materially not-so-rich life that offers him solace and contentment, obviously the choice will be the latter. This leads to the conclusion that the present day world is paying a heavy price for buying discontentment. There is no point in struggling hard to keep ourselves remain discontented.

Man has progressed very much in the external world. The scientific advancements that man has made are indeed quite surprising. But the pity is that in spite of all advancements, man has become more inhuman. What is the use of man's acquiring the whole world if in the process he becomes more and more inhuman? The reason for such a plight is that man has so far been looking outwards. Man has been seeking joy and happiness from things outside. This outward search has only eluded man from finding any meaning in life. Ancient sages and seers of India have formulated a precise science that shows the path to realize the meaning behind human life. This ancient science contained in the vast spiritual literature of India does not ask man to run away from material prosperities and mundane responsibilities. It teaches man how to live a meaningful life amidst material prosperity, without becoming a slave to the material world. It teaches man how to look inward for the great treasures that will give meaning to life.

India, with its rich cultural tradition, has a lot to offer to the humanity as a whole and to the business community in particular on the ways of leading a happy, contented and meaningful life. India is the one country where thousands of great souls have been born in every generation and they have shown to mankind the way to lead a meaningful life. I have drawn a lot from the thoughts of great seers and saints of India that are contained in the spiritual and moral literature of India. The Hindu spiritual literature is so vast that there is no branch of knowledge that is left uninvestigated. By the way, Hinduism is not a religion in the strict sense of the word. It is not a set of principles laid down by any single person. It is non-prophetic in the sense that it is not rooted in the historicity of one person and one doctrine like all other religions of the world. Very many great scholars have contributed to the knowledge pool of Hinduism that are based on eternal principles and values of life that hold good for all persons, for all time and at all places.

Since effectively managing the human resources has become more and more important for the success of an organization, the role played by leaders is vital for any organization. Many research findings indicate that the role of the CEO has a greater impact than any other factor for the success of an organization. For a CEO to be a successful and effective leader, it is imperative that he should have certain inborn and/or acquired qualities that will stand him in good stead in steering the organization to greater heights amidst the hectic competition that prevails in business. This book puts in a nutshell the essence of Indian ethos for the benefit of business leaders world over. It will open up their minds to a new dimension and will stand as a good companion to them in their journey of managing business for the betterment of the world, without they themselves getting caught in the web of materialistic ideologies and losing their precious life time. A leader is first a human being and then comes his role as the head of the group or organization that he/she leads. Hence, the leader should be one who has imbibed human values and who gives top priority to values. A person who assigns greater importance to human values will not compromise ethical and moral conduct for anything else. The wisdom of great seers that are reproduced in this book will expose the reader to the finer aspects of human values that will make one a great human being which in turn will make him/her become an effective leader, understanding the art of becoming contented, the art of remaining calm amidst chaos, the art of perfecting human relationship and remaining blissful throughout, radiating happiness towards all those whom he/she comes into contact.

Hinduism was first known by the term *'Sanathana Dharma'*. The word *'Sanathana'* means eternal. The word *'Dharma'* refers to the values of life that sustain. The concept of *Dharma* is special to Indian way of life. It has acquired such an all pervading significance that it defies precise definition. There is no word that is equivalent to the word *'Dharma'* in any language of the world. Hindu scriptures speak profusely on *Dharma*. They expect every individual to follow *Dharma* as a way of life. *Dharma* can be defined as the law of right living. The word 'right' deserves contemplation. 'Right' living should be one that is time-tested, that is acceptable to all who are rational in their approach, that is good to all living beings, that secures happiness in life and at the same time liberates man from all bondages, that makes man realize the purpose of his life on the earth, that makes man realize the inner and hidden meanings of life and to lead a purposeful life. The essentials of *Sanathana Dharma* lie scattered in abundance throughout Indian spiritual literature. If one who is born as a human being fails to get an opportunity to go through them in one's life time, it can only be said that he/she is unfortunate. It has been my long time aspiration to share with my fellow beings the hidden treasures of moral and ethical values and the finer aspects of spiritual ideology that I happened to come across in the Indian spiritual and moral literature and this book is a result of giving shape to my aspiration.

I am very much sure that this book, which is a distillation of the noble thoughts of great Indian souls, will serve as a table-top companion to business leaders, give them useful tips, make them become and remain successful leaders in their respective domain and at the same time make them realize the value of their precious life, lead a contented, meaningful and blissful life, enjoying the virtues of having been born as a human being in this wonderful earth, without getting caught in the web of trivial issues and getting their precious life time lost in the process of managing the organizational affairs, yet leading their organizations to superlative performance.

I wish the readers an interesting read.

K. Nagarajan

Acknowledgements

This small book is the result of decades of my yearning and contemplation to give the readers of Indian spiritual and value system, an insight into the hidden, subtle aspects of Indian spiritual and moral literature that are known for their contents. In my effort towards achieving this task, I had to go through volumes and volumes of ancient spiritual literary works and at times I stood spell bound on knowing the priceless wisdom of a great many seers and saints who graced this country with their presence and whose uttering still remain valid, standing the test of time. I sincerely believe that I have been fortunate enough to get exposed to their wisdom for which I will remain ever grateful to those great souls who have contributed to the vast pool of knowledge about which India can feel proud of.

In my life's journey, I happened to come across many selfless personalities who had been leading a purposeful life and who kept very low profile, remaining humble to the core. I could unlock the secret behind their simple, yet great living by correlating their vision of life with the great teachings of Indian spiritual literature and could derive a wealth of insights into the Indian Ethos and values. I am indebted to these great souls for ever.

Editors of IUP Publications(formerly ICFAI University Press), Hyderabad, Organisational Management journal, Palghat and HRD Times, Chennai have been kind enough to permit me to make use of the contents of my following articles that appeared in their journals. I wish to record my sincere thanks to the editors of these journals for having given their consent.

'Yoga for Stress Management–Prescriptions of Patanjali Maharishi', published in EFFECTIVE EXECUTIVE, January, 2005.

'Indian Wisdom on Human Behaviour and its superiority over Transactional Analysis', published in HRM REVIEW, May, 2005.

'Need Hierarchy – An Indian perspective', published in ORGANISATIONAL MANAGEMENT, Vol: XIX, No: 3, October – December, 2003.

'The relevance of Chanakya's wisdom for contemporary executives', published in ORGANISATIONAL MANAGEMENT, Vol: XX, No: 1, April – June, 2004.

'The way to work – Reminiscences from Gitanjali', published in ORGANISATIONAL MANAGEMENT, Vol: XX, No: 3, October – December, 2004.

'Maslow's self actualization need and the vision of Subramania Bharathi', published in ORGANISATIONAL MANAGEMENT, Vol: XXII, No: 1, April – June, 2006.

'Level-5 Leadership and the wisdom of Thirukkural', published in ORGANISATIONAL MANAGEMENT, Vol: XXIV, No: 1, April – June, 2008.

'Locus of control', published in HRD TIMES, Vol: 6, No: 7, July-2004.

'Stress Management – Prescriptions of Yoga Vasishta', published in HRD TIMES, Vol: 8, No: 6, June-2006.

'Bhishma in Modern Management', published in HRD TIMES, Vol: 9. No: 3, March, 2007.

Last but not the least, I must thank Dr. R.C. Gupta, Director (academic) and Mr. Saumya Gupta, Managing Director, New Age International (P) Limited, Publishers, New Delhi, who have reposed their faith in my writings and who have come forward readily to publish my books.

K. Nagarajan

Contents

Of all mobile creatures, those that have two legs are superior. Amongst two-legged creatures, those that are regenerate are superior. Amongst those that are regenerate, they that are possessed of wisdom are superior. Amongst those that are possessed of wisdom, they that have succeeded in acquiring knowledge of the soul are superior. Amongst those that are possessed of knowledge of soul, they that are endued with humility are superior.

—The Mahabharata

CHAPTER 1

The Greatness of Humility

This expansive world, how little I know of it.
—Rabindranath Tagore

1. INTRODUCTION

The one quality that stands apart in great leaders is 'humility'. 'The more you know, the less humble you will become', says an Indian proverb. Jim Collins, the management expert who spent over 20 years in trying to understand how some companies are able to sustain superlative performance has finally come to the conclusion, after extensive research work, that it is Level 5 leadership that has acted as the catalyst to take companies to truly great heights. In his article *"Level 5 leadership: The Triumph of Humility and Fierce Resolve"** he brings forth that according to his research study, executives who possess qualities of extreme humility and intense professional will act as catalysts for the statistically rare event of transforming a good company into a great one. He asserts for sure that 'good – to great' transformations don't happen without Level 5 leaders at the helm.

2. ROLE OF CEO

Jim Collins narrates in his article that the objective set before his research team was to find out as to whether a good company can become a great one and if so how? He says that he had given his research team explicit instructions to down play the role of top executives in their analyses so that they won't slip into the simplistic thinking of either 'credit the leader' or 'blame the leader'. In spite of trying ignore the role of top executives, the study has come out strongly in favour of top executives and the research

---

* Jim Collins, *"Level 5 Leadership: The triumph of humility and fierce resolve"*, Harvard Business Review, July–August, 2005.

team is said to have come to the consensus that the role of the top executives could not be ignored even if the team wanted to and that there is something consistently unusual about the top executives. All successful organizations were found to have had a Level 5 leader at the helm during the period of transition and the absence of Level 5 leaders was found to have led the organizations to doldrums. Thus, the importance of the Chief Executive has been proved once again beyond doubt. The existence of Level 5 leaders in companies that have been transformed from good to great is an empirical finding and not an ideological one.

3. WHO IS A LEVEL 5 LEADER?

Having heard Collins say that it is Level 5 leaders who have transformed organizations, there arises the curiosity to know who this Level 5 leader really is. Collins defines Level 5 leader by a simple formula as, "Humility + Will = Level 5". Level 5 leaders are dual in their nature – modest, but willful; shy but fearless. Their Outward modesty cannot be taken as a sign of their inner weakness. In fact, they have very strong professional will, though they are very modest at the same time. Collins quotes personalities like Darwin Smith, CEO of Kimberly – Clark, Colman M. Mockler, CEO of Gillette and the like who are humble but strong willed personalities who steered their organizations to great heights. Collins sketches the hierarchy of leadership levels as under:

Level 5

Executive

(Paradoxical combination of personal humility plus professional will)

↑

Level 4

Effective leader

(Commitment to the pursuit of a clear and compelling vision)

↑

Level 3

Competent manager

(Organizes people and resources towards effective and efficient pursuit of objectives)

↑

Level 2

Contributing team leader
(Contributes to the achievement of group objectives)

↑

Level 1

Highly capable individual
(Contributes through talent, knowledge, skills and good work habits)

The attributes of a Level 5 leader given by Collins are reproduced below:

Personal humility	Professional will
Demonstrates a compelling modesty shunning public adulation; never boastful.	Creates superb results, a clear catalyst in the transition from good to great.
Acts with quiet, calm determination; relies principally on inspired standards, not inspiring charisma, to motivate.	Demonstrates an unwavering resolve to do whatever must be done to produce the best long-term results, no matter how difficult.
Channels ambition into the company, not the self; sets up successors for even more greatness in the next generation.	Sets the standard of building an enduring great company; will settle for nothing less.
Looks in the mirror, not out the window, to apportion responsibility for poor results, never blaming other people, external factors, or bad luck.	Looks out the window, not in the mirror, to apportion credit for the success of the company – to other people, external factors, and good luck.

On the question whether Level 5 leaders are born or bred, Collins' frank acceptance is that the question remains to be answered. So far, so good. A look at the above attributes indicates the following personality traits of Level 5 leaders.

Modesty
Shunning public adulation
Non-boast fullness
Calm, but strong resolve
Selfless determination to lift the organisation
Grooming of successors
Accepting responsibility and avoiding blaming others/bad luck
Setting high standards and working towards it
Passing on credits for success to others

All the above traits stem forth from two qualities that are very fundamental. They are 'Humility' and 'Egolessness'. In a way, these two are interrelated. If one is humble, he can not be egoistic. If one is not egoistic, he will accommodate others' views, he will accept his faults, he will pass on due credit to others, he won't boast himself of having done anything great. In other words, he will be a humble, lovable personality. A strong resolve of a person to do good to the organization, when combined with his personal humility will make him a Level 5 leader. We are now drawn to the logical stand that the CEO has to be, above all, a humble person, besides whatever knowledge, skills and qualifications he possesses, for him to turn out to be successful in transforming the organization from either from bad to good or from good to great. Thus, humility is found to be one of the foremost personality traits required of a leader.

Let us see in the following pages as to what the ancient Indian wisdom, known for its richness, has to say on humility, the one factor that makes a lot of difference.

4. WISDOM OF *THIRUKKURAL* ON HUMILITY

Thirukkural, the book of wisdom is a 2000 years old classic. It has universal appeal and it manifests the ancient innate wisdom on human values and social life. It is a perennial source of knowledge based on rational ethics and scientific outlook.

Let us go through some of the verses of *Thirukkural* that has in them the essence of leadership qualities required of successful leaders, which in simple, crisp and clear terms brings forth the essential leadership qualities that Jim Collins has established after years of strenuous study.

Thirukkural puts forth emphatically the greatness of humility as under:

The great are always humble, while the mean
will boast in self admiration.

—Verse 978, Thirukkural

The humble person is stated to be great. By being humble, a leader does not appear belittled in the eyes of his colleagues and subordinates. On the contrary, he gains strength, credibility and respect. He becomes 'great'.

The quality of humility stems from the understanding that what does one know is a drop and what is not known is an ocean. A good leader will have all the humility to learn from others because he acknowledges that he does not have answers for all issues. He never boasts of knowledge, though he may really be highly knowledgeable. He will be modest to the core. Great souls are always humble; they never boast any pride. They keep a low profile because they know their smallness before the mighty existence. The words of Albert Einstein bring to the fore the immensity of the universe before which the entire humanity stands nothing.

The harmony of natural law which reveals an intelligence of such superiority that compared with it all the systematic thinking and acting of human beings is an utterly insignificant reflection........

There are immensely vast stretches of time and of space and humanity exists like as excrescence confined to a few metres depth on the skin of the earth...... What is humanity in the midst of this immensity? No one can fail to appreciate the vastness, intricacy of the whole structure of the universe. — *Albert Einstein.*

Great minds think alike. While Albert Einstein, one of the greatest scientists the world has seen, stands spell-bound and feels humble to the core before the immensity of the Universe, the mind of Kahil Gibran, the mystical poet and philosopher feels humble in its own way.

I am ignorant of absolute Truth. But, I am humble before my ignorance and there lies my honour and my reward.

— *Kahlil Gibran.*

Dr. S. Radhakrishnan, the Indian philosopher and statesman, who is considered to be one of the most influential scholars of comparative religion and philosophy, is true when he says that what we know is only a tiny fraction of the Universe and this realization will make one become humble to the core however knowledgeable one may considered to be in terms of materialistic knowledge that one possesses.

The ultimate questions are too deep or mysterious for science. We should recognize that we understand and control only a tiny fraction of the universe. — *Dr. S. Radhakrishnan.*

Thirukkural puts it in a nutshell saying that it is stupidity if one thinks that he knows everything.

It is nothing but stupidity if one thinks
that he knows everything.

— *Verse 844, Thirukkural*

The greatness of humility as a human virtue is further brought out by *Thirukkural* as below:

Humility earns lasting fame, grace and wisdom;
waywardness casts gloom and darkness.

— *Verse 121, Thirukkural*

Humility is virtue all round;
it adds richness to wealth.

— *Verse 125, Thirukkural*

Humility will bring success; it will also be
a wise man's weapon against his foes.

—*Verse 985, Thirukkural*

By being humble, a leader is endowed with the right mind-set to correctly judge the opponent's strengths and his own weaknesses. He is in a position to carry out a more realistic SWOT analysis, thus taking advantage of a given situation and steering his organization in the right direction.

As a consequence of the virtue of humility, a leader (a Level 5 leader, according to Collins) will not pass the blame on others. As Collins put it, they look in the mirror and not out the window to apportion responsibility for poor results. One who makes a sincere self-assessment and corrects his mistakes first will not jump to wrong conclusions, blaming others. For accepting one's own mistakes, one has to be first of all, a simple, genuine and humble human being. Let us see what *Thirukkural* has to say on this.

He who corrects his own flaws first
before finding fault with others, is a good leader

—*Verse 436, Thirukkural*

5. PERSONAL HUMILITY AND PROFESSIONAL WILL — THE TWO SIDES OF A SAME COIN

Collin's Level 5 leader is humble, but firm. Humility does not mean cowardice. A humble leader will be firm when it comes to achievement. He will not budge to pressures when it comes to safeguarding the organisation's interests. He will have calm and strong resolve to achieve. Level 5 leaders, according to Collins, have such intense will that they simply would not give in. Calm and strong resolve to handle issues is aptly brought out by *Thirukkural* in the following verse.

Firmness in principles and a serene look
are greater than a mountain.

—*Verse 124, Thirukkural*

Effective leaders set their mind on target and walk through relentlessly towards it, unmindful of criticisms.

Collins quote the example of Darwin Smith, a Level 5 leader and the CEO of Kimberly – Clark who turned it into the leading consumer paper products company in the world, beating its rivals Scott paper and Procter & Gamble. Smith did so by first selling the mills of Kimberly – Clark, since the company's traditional core business of producing coated paper was reduced to mediocrity and he thought that the company would find it difficult to face world class competitors like Procter & Gamble. He diverted all the sale proceeds into consumer business, with investments in brands like Huggies, Diapers and Kleenex tissues. Though his move was criticized by the business media as well as by Wall Street analysts, Smith was unmoved by the cynical criticisms. His single-minded devotion to the task he had set before him made Kimberly-Clark take over Scott Paper and beat Procter & Gamble in six out of eight product categories. This study of Jim Collins gives a classic example of the quality of professional will ignoring criticisms from all quarters, of a Level 5 leader. *Thirukkural* speaks of will power and self-determination to accomplish results in no uncertain terms.

> *Total involvement in a task and the will-power*
> *to perform, lead to success, the way one targets*
>
> *—Verse 666, Thirukkural*

Thus, humility and determination to achieve go together with effective leaders. They are not opposite qualities. In fact, they are complementary.

6. EGOISM VERSUS HUMILITY

All said and done, one would be curious to know what makes a person humble. Yes. You guessed it correct. It is dropping of one's ego. If one is egocentric, one can not be humble. Indian religious scriptures are full of instances where dropping of one's ego is being stressed as the one thing that a person should do (or at least attempt to do) in his life to realize the Truth behind existence. One who drops his ego in toto gets immersed with existence, becomes one with existence and for him there is no difference between the various forms of existence that an ordinary human being may perceive. For him, existence is one and not many. The different names and forms are for those who have not yet dropped their ego in full. But, dropping ego in toto is easier said than done. It might be possible for those chosen few who are liberated souls. It may not be possible for all. But one whose ego is at its lower ebb will be better placed to be a humble personality. The futility of carrying ego with us will be evident once we understand what ego really is and how it takes shape. The drawback with man is that man ordinarily lives as an ego, separate from the whole. Man wants to retain a separate identity. He wants to be somebody. That is why all the names and forms exist. Man is in the continuous process of defining himself as to who he is – like defining oneself as a CEO, as a doctor, lawyer, engineer, professor, industrialist, philosopher, saint, head of the family, husband of such and such person, father of such and such person and the list is endless. Man continues to define himself for the very simple reason that he does not know who he really is. Man is not able to know who he is. So, he starts assuming false definitions. In a way, it helps man to escape from reality, to shut his eyes to reality which is unknown and to dwell more and more on things that are unreal. So, man creates artificial arbitrary identity. He will know that it is artificial, false and meaningless only when he is bold enough to accept that he does not know who he really is.

Some of the uttering of enlightened personalities and revelations of scriptures will show what it becomes when ego is dropped. Let us go through some of them.

Ego is nothing but the center of all non-essential possessions that you have. Ego is nothing but the accumulated 'my' and 'mine' – my house, my car, my prestige, my religion, my scripture, my character, my morality, my family, my heritage, my tradition. All these 'my's' and 'mine's' go on getting accumulated; they become crystallized as the ego. —*Osho*

Yes. We keep on feeding our ego since birth. Ego comes along with success; ego comes along with power; ego comes along with wealth. As man goes after material possessions and goes after achieving power, his ego gets more and more strong. Ego is so subtle that a person will become egoistic without his knowing that he has become egoistic.

I teach contentment. And the basic principle of contentment is to drop your ego. Don't think for a single moment, 'To be or not to be'. Just not to be is the rule. What have you gained by trying to be? Just for a change, try not to be and you will be amazed. The moment you are not, there is contentment, there is silence, there is beauty and there is bliss.

—*Osho*

Indian spiritual teachings are full of instances where surrender to the Almighty is considered to be the last stage of perfection in the pursuit of Truth. Surrender refers to the surrender of ego and taking refuge in God. In the Bhagavad Gita, Lord Krishna explains to Arjuna several meditation techniques to reach the Almighty through 700 verses in 18 chapters. At the end of it, Arjuna says, "Krishna, I am more confused than I was when you started explaining. Please tell the technique that is better and quicker that I can follow." To this Lord Krishna says to Arjuna, "I have explained all methods to you; now, simply surrender everything to me. Surrender to me and I will liberate you..." Through this message Lord Krishna reveals to the world that surrender is the final and ultimate technique to reach an egoless state so that one can get liberated.

Ego is the biggest enemy of humans

—Rig veda

The minimum qualification for (getting) divine grace is surrender of ego

—Satya Sai Baba

Surrender is the only way to freedom; surrender means surrender of ego......; Remember ego can create misery; ego can create anguish; ego can create hate; ego can create jealousy. Ego can never become a vehicle for the divine; it can never become the passage for the beyond..........; The ultimate enlightenment means the ultimate dissolution of the ego, the ultimate disappearance of the individual......; When your ego is no more, only then you will know who you are.

—Osho

No vision of Truth or no vision of God is possible without annihilating the ego.

—Swami Sivananda

To Him shall I attain when my ego dies.

—Chandogya Upanishad

One can surrender his ego only if he is very humble, child-like, accepting everything as it comes, not demanding anything, putting forth every possible effort in this material world in his realm of activity but at the same time surrendering everything to the will of the Almighty. This is the state of disposition that the Bhagavad Gita induces every aspirant to reach and if a leader happens to be one who falls in line with the aspirations of the Bhagavad Gita, he will be a perfect fit to become an effective leader. Being egoless, he will have all the qualities required of a leader to take the organization to greater heights.

Thus, humility and annihilation of ego go hand in hand. One can not be egoistic and still humble. Collins brings into account one Level 5 leader saying, "There are a lot of people in this company who could do my job better than I do". It is such utmost modesty that distinguishes effective leaders from the rest. The study team of Jim Collins noted the presence of gargantuan ego of the top executives that contributed to the demise or continued mediocrity of companies. None other than *Thiruvalluvar* is capable of putting the findings of Collins in apt words. But mind it, the word of *Thiruvalluvar* are more than 2000 years old.

Boasting pride, disregarding limitations and inadaptability are sure norms leading fast to destruction

—Verse 474, Thirukkural

Finally, let us go through a beautiful poem from *Sukra Neeti* that at its end makes an impressive remark on the ill effects of pride

Old age destroys beauty
Hope destroys patience
Death destroys life
Anger destroys fortune
Serving a wicked person destroys good qualities
Lust destroys shyness
Pride destroys everything.

—*Shukra Neeti*

7. CONCLUSION

Humility is a great quality to be possessed by all individuals. It is more so, if the individual happens to be a team leader. The more humble a leader is, the more accessible he becomes to his team members. When a leader is easily accessible to his team members, he gains their confidence and the level of communication will improve substantially. Free and fair communication between a leader and his team members will solve all interpersonal problems and an atmosphere of mutual trust will prevail in the organization, which will go a long way in effective team building. For all these things to happen, the leader should be one who has a humble disposition and is free from pride of any kind.

The person who is satisfied by listening to his/her shortcomings and does not get annoyed, but tries to know more of them from the critics and gets rid of those deficiencies, who does not become over joyous on listening to his praise, but maintains calm and thinks that he has the responsibility of being more and more elevated as compared to others is a wise person. It is such person who leads others.

—Sukhra Neeti

2

CHAPTER

The Art of Listening

If there is nectar in poison, it should be extracted.
—Chanakya Neeti

1. INTRODUCTION

Only a good listener can be a great leader. Listening won't happen if one is mentally engaged. Most of the time people are mentally engaged though they may appear to be otherwise. You can be receptive to the ideas of the person talking to you only if you are not otherwise engaged mentally. But, this happens very rarely since people are almost always mentally engaged. At the background of their mind, some or other issue is always present. And if you analyze the issues that dominate your mind, you will find that they are all issues concerned with your own welfare. In other words, it will be all selfish motives that will be present at the background. They may take different names and forms. If you can peep through your thought process, you will find that always, issues that support your self-interest will gain greater importance. This is so for all human beings, except for those who are gifted with a great heart that yearns for the welfare of all living beings. Man is basically self-centered. You will be interested in anything that offers you a comfort zone. You will be against those issues that disturb your comfort zone. If you observe keenly, at the background of your mind there will be present thoughts about how to strengthen your comfort level and how to overcome those issues that disturb your comfort zone. With the mind always remaining preoccupied with self-centered thoughts, listening rarely happens. A listening mind has become hard to find. But, it is one of the prerequisites of a leader. Whether in the material world or in the metaphysical world listening happens only when the mind is tranquil, free from any engagement.

Most the interpersonal problems are the result of people misunderstanding one another. We quite frequently come across people complaining that their views are not heard or not understood correctly. An empty vessel can be filled. A vessel that is already full can not receive any further. It has to overflow. Similar is the case of listening. When the mind is preoccupied, only pseudo listening happens. It is pretending to be listening rather than really listening. A careful observation will reveal the presence of pseudo listening at many places, between peers as well as between superiors and subordinates. Pseudo listening happens when a person appears (or pretends) to be listening while his mind is engaged in some other thing. Pseudo listening will be evident, especially when people are in conflict. When in conflict, active listening never happens. People in conflict are always busy in formulating responses, without listening to the opponent's views. The obvious result will be a deadlock.

If I am already filled with my own thoughts, I won't have room for others' views. Others may express their views sincerely; but they won't enter and get registered in me. Listening has become a forgotten art. If we introspect, we will find that most of us are so busy that we expect only people to hear what we say and we have forgotten how to listen. Hence, a leader must be a very good listener. But for this, one can never become an effective leader. Thus, it all boils down to keeping the mind free from occupation and keeping it as a clean slate that becomes the first thing to be achieved for effective listening to follow. Jiddu Krishnamurthy, one of the noted philosophers and spiritual leaders of India has the following to say on the need for a tranquil mind.

When the mind is agitated, questioning, worrying, dissecting, analyzing, there is no understanding. When there is the intensity to understand, the mind is obviously tranquil. — *J. Krishnamurthy*

2. WHY SHOULD A LEADER BE A GOOD LISTENER?

All subordinates want their boss to be good listeners. If the boss is not a good listener, he informally sends the message, 'I am not for you', with the result, communication between the boss and his subordinates will suffer. Good leaders don't merely hear. They listen with all sincerity. They don't listen with an intention to shoot out a reply. They listen to understand – to understand the difficulties, expectations, concerns and yearnings of their peers and subordinates. A leader achieves the organizational goal through the active and willing cooperation of his subordinates and for this to happen the subordinates should be satisfied with their leader's attitude towards them. A satisfied and contented workforce is a very great strength for any organization and the simple formula to make the work force satisfied is to listen to them actively, compassionately.

The one who listens to the difficulties of his people keeps them satisfied.

—559, Chanakya Sutram

Once a leader has perfectcd the art of listening, it will stand him in good stead. *Thirukkural* considers the quality of listening as a great wealth that one can possess. It further goes on to add that once a person acquires this wealth, it will aid him/her acquire other forms of wealth. In an organizational context, if a leader possesses this rare skill of active listening, the leader can be deemed to have acquired a great leadership quality that will help him/her steer the organization to greater heights. The couplet of *Thirukkural* reads as under:

The gift of good listening is a basic wealth that acquires other forms of wealth and hence is the best of wealth.

—Verse 411, Thirukkural

3. ATTRIBUTES OF A GOOD LISTENER

A leader should keep his mind empty, free from any other thoughts while listening. Only then he will be able to grasp and absorb whatever is spoken to him. Withdrawing the thoughts and disengaging the mind from wandering in other domains while listening can be done by conscious effort. But it will be a very difficult task and it is more said than done. All the distortions in communications and all the inter personal misunderstandings that we come across are due to the simple reason that real listening does not take place. If the leader is not very much concerned with the speaker, not really interested in the well being of the speaker, he can not be really inclined to listen. His efforts to pull back the wandering mind are more likely to end up with failure. But, it will be a very easy task if the leader is sincerely interested in the well-being of the speaker. Thus, finally it gets reduced to having qualities like compassion, empathy, receptiveness, modesty, egolessness, impartiality, magnanimity etc., that makes one a good listener.

Compassion

A person can be a good listener only if he has got concern for others' welfare which does not come that easily. For this, one should be compassionate towards the whole of humanity. Without being compassionate one can not listen to others' views sincerely.

A compassionate leader will not consider man as a commodity, as a mere factor of production. He will be able to see divinity in every human being. He will respect, revere and worship the manifestation of divinity in every human being. And only such a person will be compassionate towards all his fellow beings by default. He will not be compassionate only towards those selected few whom he considers good and ignore others. A compassionate person is so tranquil, so genuine, so child-like that he will be in love with the whole existence. He can not divide persons into groups – good and bad, lovable and not lovable etc. His compassion will be unconditional and universal. Such a person will adopt Management by fellowship rather than Management by objectives or Management by results.

Attempting to learn the so called 'Listening tips' taught by personality trainers can not be of any real use unless a person feels companionate towards the person who speaks to him. Let us see what Indian wisdom has to say on compassion.

There is no austerity equal to peaceful and serene mind and there is no happiness equal to contentment. In the same way, there is no disease like lust and covetousness and there is no greater religion and virtue like sympathy, compassion, kindness or mercy.

—Chanakya Niti

Abandon the religion which is without compassion and mercy.

—Chanakya Niti

The first step in spiritual life is to have compassion. A person who is kind and loving never needs to go searching for God. God rushes toward any heart that beats with compassion. It is God's favourite place.

—Mata Amritanandamayi

Thus, Indian wisdom places compassion as the essence of any religion. It goes to the extent of even saying that there is no greater religion like compassion. As said earlier, a compassionate person will be compassionate towards all living beings. The following *sloka* used for daily chanting by spiritual seekers of India is an invocation for harmony and blessings for all.

Lokah Somasta Sukhino Bhavantu
(May all beings be happy)
Om Shanthi, Shanthi, Shanthi.
(Peace, peace, peace unto all beings)

Empathy

As we know, empathy is the quality of appreciating others' feelings by looking at issues from their point of view. This will help one to get a good grasp of the problem and to take decisions that are not biased towards anybody. When somebody talks to me, I can create confidence in him only if I feel empathic towards him. That will bring about an atmosphere of friendliness and the person will feel at home. Only in such an environment real conversation can take place. Empathy is an important personal virtue required for discerning others' feelings. Without being empathic one can only have a partial, one-sided view of any issue. All dialogues in which the persons involved do not feel empathic towards each other will only be a set of monologues. When one knows that the person with whom he speaks is listening to him sincerely with empathy, he will open out and vent his feelings and views without any shade of hesitation. Only then there will be a real and meaningful dialogue between the two. People feel at ease only in the presence of those who lend their ears wholeheartedly.

Thirukkural makes things clear when it says that there is no use of any amount of wisdom that one has gained if he does not feel painful at the pain of others. This is exactly what empathy is all about. I will be able to feel the pain that the other person undergoes only if I put myself in the other person's position and look at the issue.

What does a man from wisdom gain
if he pines not at others' pain?

—Verse 315, Thirukkural

Thiruvalluvar is so universal in his vision that he feels empathic not only towards human beings, but towards all beings on the earth. This is his greatness. Empathy is a quality that springs from the fountain of love and love knows no boundary. It is like fragrance and it will spread all round, towards all beings.

One should not harm other living beings on the earth
by things known to be injurious to self.

—Verse 318, Thirukkural

Good listeners don't jump into conclusions. Good listeners don't listen with the intent to reply; they listen with the intent to understand. And this can happen only if the person who listens to the other feels empathic towards him. Communication will not suffer where there is empathy. Thus, a leader can be an effective leader if he possesses the quality of empathy as it provides the platform for active listening.

Receptiveness

One can be a good listener only if he/she is receptive to the ideas, views and opinions of others. He/she must receive others' views without any kind of prejudice whatsoever. Good listeners are open to the views, ideas and opinions from wherever they come and whosoever offer them. Only an empty vessel can receive. A vessel that is already full will only overflow. Hence, however knowledgeable a leader may be, he must listen to others' views with an empty mind, with an ardent desire to know anything that is not known to him. Indian ethical and spiritual literatures contain many quotes which put emphasis on the importance of being receptive to the views and opinions of others.

Let Noble thoughts come to us from every side.

—1:89:1, Rig Veda

Reasonable suggestion even of children should be accepted.

—167, Chanakya Sutram

To perceive clearly the truth in any matter
Spoken by anybody is wisdom.

—Verse 423, Thirukkural

Good suggestions of even a child should be accepted;
Good conduct should be learnt even from an enemy;
And gold be picked up even from the dirt.

—2:214, Manu Smriti

Nothing is difficult to those who act
on the advice of the wise, after careful thought.

—Verse 462, Thirukkural

An effective leader will be receptive to the views of all concerned and will not apply mental filters while he receives others' views.

Modesty

The more and more a person knows, the more and more he realizes that there remains a lot yet to be known. Hence, knowledge, in the true sense, should only breed modesty. If one does not become modest despite his having learnt many a thing, it only points out to the fact that whatever he has learnt are no worth their salt. One who is modest automatically becomes receptive – receptive to the views and opinions of all, because, he knows that the pearls of wisdom may remain hidden in any place. Indian wisdom on modesty is worth remembering and cherishing for ever.

There are none who know everything;
Be modest; the chisel will break the rock which
a huge sledge hammer can not.

—189, Neethi Neri

Compare yourself, not with those
below you (in knowledge),
but with those above.

—190 Neethi Neri

It is nothing but stupidity if one thinks
that he knows everything.

—Verse 844, Thirukkural

Heeding to Advice

The team that a leader heads might consist of members of different cadre, calibre and skills. It is quite likely that some of the team members may be more knowledgeable and more skillful in certain functional/operational areas of business than the leader. A leader can not master the intricacies of every functional and operational area of business. In a way, it even need not be. No doubt the leader should have the basic knowledge about all aspects of his business. But, getting to know the nuts and bolts of everything will cost one the entire life time. How can the affairs be managed and the business run under such conditions? The answer is simple and obvious. A leader manages by getting every one of his team member to participate in the process by giving them suitable direction and by ensuring that the efforts put forth by all the team members are in tune with the organizational requirement. The leader can play his role effectively if he listens to the team members and take their advices and suggestions wherever required. An effective leader will not hesitate to heed to the advice of others. Now, let us see what Indian scriptures have to say on this.

The person who is satisfied by listening to his/her shortcomings and does not get annoyed but tries to know more of them from the critics and gets rid of those deficiencies, who does not become over joyous on listening to his praise but maintains calm and thinks that he has the responsibility of being more and more elevated as compared to others is a wise person. It is such person who leads others. The common people emulate such enlightened ones.

—3: 303, 308, Sukhra Neeti

Learning the intricacies of tasks from experts
is the way to execute such tasks

—Verse 677, Thirukkural

But the crux of the issue is that one can not develop these skills simply for the sake of improving one's listening skills. One has to imbibe these skills. And that can not happen unless the listener is genuinely interested in the well-being of the speaker. If the listener is an altruist, listening skills will develop in him on their own; it may not be needed of him to take extra efforts to horn his/her listening skills.

4. CONCLUSION

Some of the tips normally given in training sessions and workshops on imparting learning skills are as below:

Develop a desire to learn

Always let the other person do most of the talking

Don't interrupt

Learn active listening

Ask for clarification if needed

Get used to 'listening' for non-verbal messages (body languages)

But the crux of the issue is that one can not develop these skills merely by training. One's personality should be disposed towards that. One has to imbibe these skills. And that can not happen unless the listener is genuinely interested in the well being of the speaker. The leader has to be an altruist. An altruist will have the innate passion to listen to others because he is genuinely interested in the welfare of others. For him, active listening is a way of life. An effective leader will be an altruist and can not remain without listening actively to others.

Let go anger
Let go pride

....

....

Anger is like a chariot careering wildly.
He who curbs his anger is the true charioteer;
Others merely hold the reins.

—The Dhammapada

3

CHAPTER

The Irrelevance of Anger

You will not be punished for your anger;
You will be punished by your anger.

—Gautama Buddha

1. INTRODUCTION

Anger has caused great damages for humanity. Many wars have been fought because a few persons who were at the helm of affairs of some countries could not control their anger. Since anger spoils rational thinking, it leads to many conflicts. Coming to a business organization, anger has the potential to harm interpersonal relationships and to block communication, thus breeding inefficiency. Anger makes the work place, a place of hatred and discontent. An effective leader knows well the ill effects of anger. He will not allow anger to overtake him and will set an example for others to emulate. A person who is angry loses his energy. An effective leader will not waste his energy in fruitless issues and anger is one such thing.

When you get angry, you lose energy through your eyes, nose, mouth, ears and every pore of your body.

—Mata Amritanandamayi

Since a person overcome by anger will lose his energy in many ways, he will be toiling hard but without any fruitful result.

"...the toil of an angry man becomes entirely fruitless...."

—Section CCC, Santi parva,
The Mahabharata

Since anger takes birth in human metabolism, its origin is very subtle. Once the seeds of anger get planted in human metabolism, it becomes part of human system and hence it becomes all the more difficult to control. This is why we come across wider prevalence of anger in work places despite many having been advocating against anger over the years. Indian wisdom does an in-depth analysis of anger and helps us understand its mechanism and provides us with effective tips to overcome it.

2. THE MECHANISM OF ANGER

The desire for objects is common for man. As desires are many and desirable objects are few, many of the desires remain unfulfilled. Unfulfilled desires lead to disappointment, which in turn breeds anger. That is why Indian scriptures point out that desire is the root cause of all pains and miseries that human beings pass through.

Lord Krishna brings out distinctly in The Bhagavad Gita as to how anger gets into a man.

When a man dwells on the objects of sense, he creates an attraction for them; attraction develops into desire and desire breeds anger.

—Verse-62, Chap. 2, The Bhagavad Gita

The causes of anger may appear to be different. It may take many shapes. But, at the root of anger we can find a disappointment – something happening against our wishes. These wishes are the expression of desire – desire for some material objects, desire for position and status, desire for some sensual pleasures, desire for some psychological comfort etc. When what we long for is not forthcoming, it triggers anger. And anger is directed towards the person whom we consider responsible for our disappointment. Thus, those who want to be anger-free should know that it is desire for fleeting things that is the root cause. Hence, anger can not be suppressed. It will be poisonous to suppress anger. The only way to avoid anger is to cut its root, viz., to be free from desires.

Desire is the root cause of all miseries.

—Gautama Buddha

Anger simply means that something in you is hurt;
some wound is there.

—Osho

3. CONSEQUENCES OF ANGER

Anger clouds the mind of a man and makes him incapable of arriving at rational decisions. When in anger, the mind is unable to perceive things correctly. When perceptions become false, the decisions turn out to be erroneous. The distinction between man and animal is that man has got the faculty of discrimination. In many other aspects, man resembles animal. The power to discriminate between good and bad, right and wrong, desirable and undesirable is what makes man superior to animals. The ability to discriminate comes from knowledge. Knowledge is nothing but the total accumulated experiences, both direct and indirect that are stored in the mind as memories. At the moment when a person is angry, his memory gets clouded and he temporarily suffers from 'loss of memory', which means that he suffers from lack of power to discriminate. Discrimination is possible only with reference to the pool of knowledge that is stored in the form of memories. Since anger prevents one to perform his actions patiently by referring to the accumulated knowledge stored in him, he starts acting irrationally. *The Bhagavad Gita* gives a perfect anatomy of the consequences of anger.

Anger induces delusion, Loss of memory; through Loss of memory, reason is shattered and loss of reason leads to destruction.

—Verse 63, Chapter 2, The Bhagavad Gita

Vidhura Neeti, another great ethical text of India speaks in the same voice of *the Bhagavad Gita.*

Desire and anger break through wisdom
just as a large fish breaks through a net of thin cords.

—Vidhura Neeti

Since anger spoils the rational behaviour of a person, his actions will be against *dharma.*

The angry man commiteth sin. The angry men killeth even his preceptors. The angry man insulteth even his superiors in harsh words. The man that is angry faileth to distinguish between what should be said and what should not. There is no act an angry man may not do, no word that an angry man may not utter.........Beholding all these faults the wise control their anger.....

—Section XXIX, Book 3, Vana Parva, The Mahabharata

Thus, anger causes great damages by way of wrong decisions and wrong actions and its effect will be more pronounced when persons who hold leadership positions in organizations succumb to anger and take wrong decisions, since such wrong decisions will have serious consequences and has the potential to bring down even great organizations.

Since a person overpowered by anger takes irrational decisions, he will not be liked by people around. He will develop more and more enemies and this will eventually make life worse for him.

Anger makes one the object of hatred, creates enemies
And brings suffering to oneself.

—Arthasashtra

Forget anger, in any case, towards any one;
Else only evil and pain will be the outcome.

—Verse 303, Thirukkural

Hatred and anger leads to unhappiness, pain and misery.

—Yajur Veda

Anger in work place has the power to make the entire environment stressful and non-conducive for smooth functioning. Another aspect of anger in organizations is its multiplier effect. It will spread from one person to another. It is like a contagious disease, affecting any one who comes across it. If the top leader of an organization is one who always feels angry at others, this will send wrong signals and subordinates down the line will also get infected by anger.

When you are angry with someone and you throw your anger on him, you are creating a chain reaction.

—Osho

Anger robs one of happiness and laughter. A leader can not lead a team to success unless he keeps his team members in good spirits. And a leader can not keep his team members in good spirits and good humour if he himself does not know how to enjoy lighter moments in life. Only those who can keep anger away can enjoy lighter moments in life.

Is there any enemy more injurious than anger
that spoils laughter and happiness?

—Verse 304, Thirukkural

4. THE EFFECT OF ANGER ON HUMAN METABOLISM

Anger spoils human metabolism and acts as the root cause for many physical and mental ailments. Anger builds up stress and the human metabolism reacts to stress. Physiologists have found out that in response to stress, the pituitary gland secretes a body chemical called Adrenocortocotropic hormone (ACTH) into the blood, which induces the adrenal gland to produce other body chemicals called Adrenaline and Norepinerphine. The release of these chemicals into the human body system gives rise to increase in blood pressure and increase in blood sugar level. Thus, the connection between mental stress and physical ailments has been established beyond doubt. It is estimated that more than 75% of all medical complaints are all stress related. Gautama Buddha had rightly said that anger will punish a person. When Buddha says, 'you will be punished by your anger', he means the negative effects that anger will bring into the body metabolism and spoil it.

Thiruvalluvar, the great saint who lived in 30 B.C., puts forth in straight terms, without leaving any scope for interpretation that the bad effects of anger can kill a person.

To safeguard oneself, let one keep away from anger;
else, he will be killed by his own anger.

—*Verse 305, Thirukkural*

Anger takes control of the person who is angry and distorts his perceptions. This is why, angry people are often found to make poor decisions. Nobody is ready to invite troubles; but anybody who succumbs to anger invites troubles for himself. Business executives are to keep anger at a safe distance if they want to enjoy their work and life. Since anger affects the mental health, business executives who get angry at their work situations fail to maintain cordial relations with their co-workers, subordinates and superiors, find fault with others and fail to follow their conscience in their behavioural pattern. It will create enemies both within and outside the organization and will bring mental unrest to the person concerned. Hence, '*Keep away from anger*' is an important *mantra* for a business executive.

5. CONCLUSION

Anger management has become one of the hot topics of leadership development programmes. In spite of much that have been said and written against anger, it is found that anger continues to prevail in the society. It is seen in every work place. It is not infrequent to come across angry bosses. In fact, it is painful to note that the word anger has almost become synonymous with the word boss. Anger can not be stopped or repressed after its seeds have been sown. Then, it is very difficult; the seed has to grow and that is natural. The wise leader will see the futility of anger. He will recognize that it is some of his unfulfilled desire that is responsible for the cause of anger in him. He knows that anger will vanish without any trace if the roots are destroyed, if he chooses to be desire-free. And that is the technique. Osho gives us another technique to get away from anger.

When you are angry, watch it. Now you are not just angry; a new element is introduced into it; you are watching it. And the miracle is that if you can watch anger, the anger disappears without being repressed.

—*Osho*

The technique suggested by Osho is one that will be useful when anger has already set in. Still it is possible to overcome it. This can be done not by suppressing it, but by watching it. It may look ridiculous. How can anger be overcome by watching it? It is not controlling. It is not repressing. It is knowing the futility of it – knowing that it has resulted as a consequence of some unfulfilled desire and observing the futility of the desire itself. It is simply standing apart from oneself and watching the ugly faces of anger, its origin, its growth, its consequences and above all its futility. Then, anger will vanish, will disappear without any trace, just as mist disappears in the presence of sunlight.

Our journey through life has been perfectly planned by infinite Love and infinite Wisdom. There can be no mistake. Every experience that comes to us is just the right experience occurring at the right time to train us in the right way. So, let us accept all that comes and never attempt to circumvent anything.

—J.P. Vaswani

CHAPTER 4

The Beauty Behind Acceptance

Give me the strength to surrender
my strength to Thy will with Love.

— Rabindranath Tagore

1. INTRODUCTION

Human mind has a peculiar nature, that of complaining. In any organization, right from the chief executive up to the employee in the lowest cadre, every one has got complaints. If the chief executive is dissatisfied with the non-cooperative attitude of the directors in the board of the company, the lowest level employee has got complaints that his immediate superior extends a much undignified treatment to him. Thus, all the members of an organization have some form of complaints or the other with regard to their working conditions and working environment. The urge to complain about others stems forth from the very nature of human mind that does not get satisfied with whatever is available and always demands more and more. There is no denying the fact that interpersonal frictions do exist among organizational members in all organizations. But, life is not all that. People join an organization to get some of their needs satisfied. Their needs differ. And the levels of satisfaction that they derive out of the same working conditions also differ. But, it will be so. After all, an organization is man-made. It is a man-made social group in which persons with different attitudes, different aims, different need patterns and different perceptions towards life join together. Hence, there are bound to be differences – difference of opinions, difference in approach to work etc., leading to interpersonal conflicts.

An organizational member is in the first place a human being and next comes his position as a member of the organization. The latter arises out of pure compulsion – a compulsion to make a living, to maintain a certain standard of living. The gifts made available to every living being are far more precious and far more valuable. If one gets entangled in the trifles of interpersonal conflicts within the organization and loses sight of the treasures that he has been gifted with, he simply allows his life to go waste. Contrary to this, if one recognizes the gifts that one has been endowed upon and knows how to rejoice at having been so fortunate to be a human being, he will remain ever joyful for having been gifted with this precious life and will remain ever thankful to the existence. Rabindranath Tagore feels thankful for the gifts that have been given to him unasked for. He touches the peak of thankfulness that every human being should possess. Such a perception will change one's attitude towards life and he will not complain about trifles like working conditions, interpersonal conflicts etc. He will remain untouched by personality clashes that have in fact done more harm for the smooth functioning of organizations.

Day by day
Thou art making me
worthy of simple, great gifts
that Thou gavest to me unasked –
this sky, and light
this body and the life and the mind......

—*Gitanjali*

Life is so precious a gift that every one should feel blissful. The gift of life is invaluable and there can be no complaints in leading a life, however unfortunate one may consider oneself to be. Once a person obtains this right perception of life, every hurdle that comes by will all be meaningless to him and this will pave way for accepting life, the precious gift of God as it is, as a *prasada* from God. (The Sanskrit word *prasada* means 'mercy'.) It is a gracious gift given by a saint, a perfect Master, an *Avatar* or a deity. It is anything edible that is first offered to a deity, a saint, a Master or an *Avatar* and then distributed to the devotees in His name. The *prasada* is considered to have the deity's blessings residing in it.

The Hindu way of life expects man to accept life and all the happenings from birth to death as a *prasada* from God.

2. TOTAL ACCEPTANCE, A GREAT QUALITY

Buddha calls acceptance by the word *'tathata'*. It is total acceptance; just accepting whatever comes and living through it silently, not being disturbed by anything, passing through all kinds of experiences unperturbed. This is possible only if one is unconnected to the happenings around, remaining simply a watchful observer. Then, one can pass through the world uncontaminated. Buddha does not advocate renouncing the world. But, he realized that renouncing the world is not required only after he himself renouncing and wandering through the forests, meeting one saint after another for years together. After Buddha experienced the truth and came back home, his wife asked him only one question. She asked Buddha, 'I have seen that you have become enlightened; you are now a transformed being; the whole world recognizes your enlightenment.......but, please tell me one thing. Whatsoever you have attained, was it not possible to attain it living here with me in this palace?' Buddha remained silent. He did not utter a world. By his silence he meant that his wife was right. He could have attained whatever he had attained by remaining in the world, by being a king, by participating in the worldly affairs and still remaining apart from the worldly activities, very much apart mentally though very much in it physically. Yes, for knowing the Truth, for knowing the hidden secrets of life, for getting enlightened about the meaning of life, it is not necessary for one to renounce life and go to the forest in search of the unknown. This is a great realization of not only the Buddha, but of all realized souls. One can be in this world, very much in this world participating in all its activities as every one else is doing and still become enlightened. This is possible by accepting everything that comes in the way, yet remaining away from this world, yet searching for the meaning in each and every incident that one comes across. Then life becomes meaningful, throbbing with energy, revealing the hidden secrets behind existence. This is the beauty behind acceptance. Accepting everything in life without any wish or hate, without any attachment or detachment will take away all the unwanted tensions that modern man undergoes from morning to night, day in and day out.

3. REMAINING RELAXED IN A WORLD OF HASTE

The pressure to earn profit, the pressure to meet competition, the pressure to sustain for long – in short, the pressure to stay above board in a world of turmoil where the one who is not on vigil will be drowned, keeps every one tense and busy always.

What is this life, if full of care
We have no time to stand and stare.

....

—Henry Davies

Present day business executives have no time to eat and sleep, leave alone standing and staring at life. Work, work and work has become the order of the day. In a world where only the fittest can survive, every one wants to prove that he is the fittest and this keeps every one always tense and on the run. The jungle rule of survival of the fittest has become the golden rule of business. The business community has somehow inherited it.

Let us leave the debate aside as to whether the rule is right or wrong. The rule has come to stay and it only promises stiffer and highly competitive days ahead. But, there is a need to stand and stare while still running after the daily chores. There is a need to still the mind and relax a while. Else, it will become only a world in which there are only mad crowds keep running, chasing a mirage. It will lead to all mental and physical illness. Tagore asks for a moment's rest to sit by the side of the Almighty. He calls it a moment's indulgence and rightly so.

I ask for a moment's indulgence
to sit by Thy side.
The works that I have in hand
I will finish afterwards.

—*Gitanjali*

A moment's rest, putting everything on hand down and remaining simply as a part of this mighty existence is a must. This will cleanse the mind of worries and will recharge one to keep pace ahead. Keeping oneself busy, maintaining tight schedules, aiming targets of tall orders are all, no doubt, part of one's job. But, occasional stop-gaps of finding rest at the feet of the Almighty is all the more required. For those who are not convinced that there exists a super power controlling every activity of the universe, it might be finding rest before the mighty existence which exists with all its might and all its wonders. For one who has known how to rest at the feet of the Almighty, all his work will become a play and he will be like a child who plays and takes a moment's rest at his mother's lap. But for this, work will only become a burden. Let us see how Tagore depicts work that lacks respite.

Away from the sight of Thy face
my heart knows no rest nor respite.
And my work becomes
an endless toil in
a shoreless sea of toil.

—*Gitanjali*

4. BECOMING AN INSTRUMENT AT THE HANDS OF THE LORD

One can be very active outwardly, remaining very calm inside, if one performs his actions without any attachment. But this mindset of finding rest at the feet of the Almighty is possible only for those who accept life as it is, as a *prasada* of God. This is possible if one realizes that he is only an instrument at the hands of the Almighty.

Don't choose; Accept life as it is in its totality.

—*Osho*

Then, all his actions will be pure, perfect and unadulterated because he understands that it is God who acts through him. Only then, work becomes worship. Tagore brings these aspects of work so vividly that his words will leave an indelible impression in the minds of readers.

This little flute of a reed
Thou hast carried over hills and dales
and hast breathed through it,
melodies eternally new.
....
....
And it shall be my endeavour
to reveal Thee in my actions,
knowing that it is Thy power
gives me strength to act.

—*Gitanjali*

Every one of us has the moral obligation to perform our duties. No doubt, one must attend to one's duties whole-heartedly. However, the word 'duty' has received undue reverence, of late. Performance of duty shall not act as a hindrance to celebrate life. Life is a celebration and anything that stands as obstacle to celebrate life should be shunned. If duty stands in between a person and his celebration of life, it only means that duty has been assigned a status that it does not deserve. Life is so precious that it can not be lost in the disguise of performing duty. It may be asked as to how a business executive, or for that matter, any body else, can neglect his duty which is his bread and butter. Yes, duty comes first. But, at the background, there must stand life, the greatest gift of God. It is like an actor who casts a role in a play. Though he performs his role perfectly on the stage, he knows for sure that he is different from the personality that he projects on the stage. If he goes to the extent of identifying himself as one of the characters in the play, it only means that he has mistaken his identity and the burden of his mistaken identity will come down heavily upon him. All the worries and mental stress of the modern man are due to his mistaken identity. Every person identifies himself as a manager, as a chief executive, as a professor, as a doctor, as an entrepreneur and the like as the case may be, forgetting that he is a human being who has adorned a role in the society. This mistaken identity is due to the undue reverence given to one's duty and this will cloud one's vision.

Tagore visualizes duty as a chain with which man binds himself. Duty is to be performed in a state of awareness that the performer is different from the 'person' behind. Such a perception will make one perform any work, however taxing it may be, in a lighter vein. Else, a person will buy burdens for a price, entangling himself with a golden handcuff in the disguise of duty. Tagore calls the one who gets himself so trapped as a prisoner.

'Prisoner, tell me, who was it
that wrought this unbreakable chain ?'
'It was I', said the prisoner, who
forged this chain very carefully.
'I thought my invincible power would hold the world
captive leaving me in a freedom undisturbed;
Thus, night and day I worked at the chain
with huge fires and cruel hard strokes.
When at last the work was done
and the links were complete and unbreakable,
I found that it held me in its grip'.

—*Gitanjali*

Becoming an instrument at the hands of God requires a total surrender, total acceptance to whatever happens. Duty can not and should not stand in between a person and his surrender to the Almighty.

5. KARMA THEORY AND ITS RELEVANCE

Karma Theory is one of the most important beliefs in Hinduism. It has been accepted by many great scholars as it provides answer to many questions that confounds men. The word *karma* denotes action. It denotes actions that bring back results. The results can occur either in the present life or in the future life. The theory of cause and effect is widely accepted by all as it is considered well founded. The doctrine of *karma* is also based on the theory of cause and effect. The theory of *karma* is to the spiritual world what the law of cause and effect to the physical world. Hinduism provides answer to the question as to why inequalities and suffering exist in the world, only through *karma* theory. Every action leads to a result. The result may be good or bad based on the quality of the deed. The law of *karma* conserves the fruits of all actions and conditions our present as well as our future lives accordingly. Every individual is an effect of his/her own infinite past. The present life of an individual is determined by the results of the past deeds. Every child is born to work out its own past deeds. According to the law of *karma*, we are the effects of our own causes. What one had done in the past decides what one is in the present life.

What one does today determines his/her tomorrow. Hinduism is based on the belief that there is a perfect universal order that sustains the universe. Since the universal order (we may call it God or Almighty or whatever) is perfect, nothing can happen without a cause. If a person suffers in the present life, no body else can be the cause except himself. He should have done something that would have led to his suffering. This is the basis of *karma* theory and it goes with Jesus Christ's words, '*whatever a man soweth, that shall he reap also*'. Every physical action of a person is a deed. His/her speech and words are deeds. Even his/her thoughts are very much deeds. Every thought, word or action generates an appropriate reaction and is weighed on the scales of eternal justice. Nobody can get away from the clutches of *karma.*

As one acts and conducts himself, so does he become. The doer of good becomes good. The doer of evil becomes evil. One becomes virtuous by virtuous action, bad by bad action.

—Maitri Upanishad

Karma not experienced does not die away
even in thousands of millions of ages.

—Verse-46, Chapter-I, Garuda Purana

The doctrine of *karma* denies the arbitrary rule of God. According to it, it is not God who rewards the virtuous and punishes the wicked. God has no role to play here. It is the virtuous who reward themselves by their own good deeds and it the sinners who punish themselves for their own wrong deeds. Thus, the responsibility lies squarely on individuals. One can not shift the blame on others.

"The past *karma* of an individual is divided into two components, viz., '*prarahdha karma*' and '*sanchita karma*'. The *prarahdha karma* is that part of one's past *karma* which is to bear fruit in the present life of an individual. The *sanchita karma* is the accumulated *karma* of the previous births which is to bear fruit in the future.

Prarahdha is that portion of the past karma which is responsible for the present body. That portion of the sanchita karma which influences human life in the present incarnation is called prarabdha. It is ripe for reaping. It cannot be avoided or changed. It is only exhausted by being experienced. You pay your past debts. Prarabdha karma is that which has begun and is actually bearing fruit. It is selected out of the mass of the sanchita karma."

—Swami Sivananda

Again, the *prarahdha karma* of an individual consists of two components – Fixed and variable. The fixed component of *prarahdha karma* is beyond our control and consists of that component of the past *karma* which determines one's parents, the family in which one must be born, the major incidents that will take place in the life of the person, the general features of the physical body that the person will eventually develop, the social and religious environments in which the person must grow etc. Thus, the family in which a person takes birth, which is a major factor that decides his/her status in life, is decided by *prarahdha karma.* That is why when one person is born in a rich family, to noble parents while another person is born in poverty, to parents without lofty ideals, Hinduism attributes the reason for such differences in birth to the *prarahdha karma* of the respective persons. The variable component of the *prarahdha karma* remains latent in the child in the form of *samskaras or vasanas* (natural habits and tendencies). The vast differences in the natural habits and tendencies of persons that we come across are thus, due to the differences in their *samskaras.* It is the variable part of the *prarahdha karma* that one can overcome by initiative and free-will. The level of success that one can achieve in diluting the effects of the variable component, however, depends upon the power of the *samskaras* and the strength of the individual's will.

Apart from *prarahdha karma and sanchita karma,* there is one more called the *aagami karma. Aagami karma* is that portion of *karma* that is created in the present life and that will be added to the *sanchita karma.* There is an interesting analogy in the vedic literature that explains the relationship between *prarahdha karma*, *sanchita karma* and *aagami karma.* There is an archer with a bundle of arrows in the quiver on his back. He has already sent an arrow and the arrow has left his hands. He is about to shoot to another arrow. The arrow that has already left the hands of the archer is *prarahdha karma.* The arrow that has been shot can not be called back. Similarly *prarahdha karma* has already made one to take life on this earth. One can not exhaust it without experiencing it. The bundle of arrows in the quiver is *sanchita karma.* It will take some more time for the arrows in the quiver to be used. *Sanchita karma* will be passed on to the individual concerned in the forthcoming lives. The result of the arrow that one is about to shoot is the *aagami karma.* To reap the fruits of one's actions, good or bad, an individual must be born again and again in the physical world. Karma theory supports reincarnation because one has to take rebirth to enjoy the fruits of his/her actions. Thus, the law of *karma* binds an individual to the cycle of birth and death.

Let us ponder over some of the greatest utterings in Indian spiritual literatures that explain karma theory.

When his body has been destroyed by fire,
his karma remains and wherever he is,
the man experiences it, be it good or bad.

—Verse-104, Chapter-VIII, Garuda Purana

Karma which has been made, whether good or evil
must inevitably be suffered;
Karma not suffered, does not fade away
in thousands of millions of ages.

—Verse-57, Chapter-V, Garuda Purana

Man must realize that there is no escape from the
consequences of one's actions.
Hence, man should shun evil deeds.

—Chapter-4, Garuda Purana

One gets the reward of one's action without fail.

—Chapter-5, Garuda Purana

The soul goes to another (fresh) body again in accordance with its past deeds (karma). It journeys in this manner till release, like a fish moving between the two banks of a river.

—Verse-12, Chapter-XI, Siva Gita

The doctrine of reincarnation provides the only plausible explanation for the seeming injustices and inequalities among men – all of whom are God's beloved children. The soul, all-perfect and ever-perfect is compelled by the law of evolution to incarnate repeatedly in progressively higher lives – retarded by wrong actions and desires and accelerated by spiritual endeavours – until self-realization and God-union are attained.

—Paramahansa Yogananda

6. NISHKAMA KARMA

It must be noted that according to Hinduism, a good *karma* is equally bad as a bad *karma* in as far as binding an individual to the birth and death cycle is concerned. Freedom from the cycle of birth and death is the ultimate objective that an *atman* should strive to achieve. Freedom from the cycle of birth and death can be achieved by adherence to the doctrine of *nishkama karma*. According to this doctrine, an individual who performs actions without attachment to their fruits is freed from the bondage of birth and death, thereby attaining a state which is beyond all suffering. According to *karma* Theory, what binds man is not action per se but man's involvement in action attracted by the fruits of action. This is because *karma* theory rests on the firm belief that it is man's attitude towards action that makes an impression on the sub-conscious mind.

If one wants not to add any further *karma* to his/her balance in the *sanchitha karma*, he/she should perform his *aagami kamas* in such a way that they are all done in the form of *nishkama karma.* What is *nishkama karma*? To understand the attributes of *nishkama karma* we need to understand the opposite, the *sakam karma* which is the action performed in expectation of something. Expectations never end. When one expectation is fulfilled, another arises and there is no end to the expectations. The mind-body complex lives on the simple principle of 'keep desiring'. Performing an action (good or bad) with expectations of results binds a person to the cycle of birth and death. Hence, those who perform *sakam karma*, simply waste their efforts irrespective of whether they perform good or bad karma. On the contrary, no effort is wasted in the path of *nishkama karma*. Every small effort is satisfying. There is always fulfillment. Frustration never happens. The formula for *nishkam karma* is : *karma minus kamana** = *nishkam karma.*

Rishi Ram Ram quotes as under as to how man does not acquire fresh *karma.*

".....Man's progress in the world is governed by his *karma* and *karma* is the result of his action. Man is born in the world to work out his *karma.* He is a wandering spirit who takes birth in the earth in suitable environment to work off his *karma*. For working off his karma, he has to do some acts, but in doing so, he gathers fresh *karma* which again necessitates his birth. Thus, the cycle of his life and death takes place. Man. However, he can work off his *karma* without gaining any fresh *karmic* load if he acts without a selfish motive, he will not acquire fresh *karma*......."

Lord Krishna tells us to remove the *kamana* factor from all our actions. When expectations are given up, there is no wasted effort. Any effort that a person makes will bring some result. And the person will be thankful for the result, whatever the result may be. He will be in a state of total acceptance – in a state of '*tathata*' as Buddha called it. There is no preconceived expectation of how the results of effort should turn out. This greatly relieves one from mental strain. Another point worth noting is that there are no obstacles (*pratyavaya*) in the path of *nishkama karma.* It seems as if the energy of the universe flows along with such a person. It is more readily available to him when compared to a man on the path of *sakam karma.* Such a person is more in harmony with the powers of nature. The end result is that a person on the path of *nishkama karma* is more effective than a person on the path of *sakam karma.*

(*kamana** means expectations).

Moreover, *nishkama karma* protects one from the fear of failures because he is prepared to accept anything that comes on the way, be it success or failure.

This is why Lord Krishna asks us to remove *kamana* from all our actions. When one removes *kamana* (desire) from all one's actions, it means that he will act without any expectations about the results. *Karma yoga* is nothing but the path of *nishkama karma* and by default, a person on the path of *karma yoga* will be peaceful happy and fearless. Such a person is bound to be highly effective and more productive. A leader, when happens to be a *karma yogi,* will be most effective in performing his organizational role.

The wise, possessed with knowledge, renouncing the fruits of their actions, become freed from the bondage of birth and death and reach that state which is beyond all evil.

—Chapter-2, Verse-51, The Bhagavad Gita

7. KARMA THEORY VIS-À-VIS KARMA YOGA

According to *karma* theory, man gets caught in the cycle of birth and death by performance of *karma* with expectations. The performance may be in words, deeds or thoughts. Having born as a human being in flesh and blood one can not refrain from performing any act.

No man can attain freedom from activity by refraining from action;
Nor can one reach perfection by merely refusing to act.

—Verse-4, Chapter-3, The Bhagavad Gita

How, then, is it to accumulate no further *karmic* load? It is by performing *karma* without any desire for the results thereof, viz., by performing *nishkama karma*.

But since those still in the body cannot entirely avoid action, in their case, abandonment of the fruit of action is considered as complete renunciation.

—Verse-11, Chapter-18, The Bhagavad Gita

We are all being dragged along by this mighty, complex world-machine. There are only two ways out of it. One is to give up all concern with the machine and stand aside – that is to give up all desire. That is very easy to say, but almost impossible to do. The other way is to plunge into the world and learn the secret of work and that is the way of karma yoga.

—Swami Vivekananda

By performing *nishkama karma*, the state of mindlessness gradually sets in. When one reaches a mindless state, he is free from the effects of actions that he/she performs though outwardly he/she may appear to be performing a lot of actions. In other words, the person becomes a *karma yogi*.

If we cultivate the spirit of detachment from results and dedication to God, we may engage in action. One who acts in this spirit is a perpetual Sanyasin. He accepts things as they come and leaves them without regret when necessary..... The chain of karma can be broken, here and now, within the flux of the empirical world. We become masters of karma by developing detachment (from results) and faith in God. .....

—Dr. S. Radhakrishnan

The purpose of Gita is to show that we are not asked to give up work in the world. We are asked to participate in the work of the world with our minds free from egoism, desire, fear etc.,

—Dr. S. Radhakrishnan

Ma Amirtanandamayi's exposition on Karma Yoga deserves to be read, reread, understood and practiced.

...... One can work without desire by doing service with the feeling that one is serving the Supreme Being in everyone....

.... Whatever work is undertaken, let it be done with one's whole being and in the spirit, "Thou alone workest" so that there may be no opportunity for affliction, distress or sorrow to creep in..... there is a stage where working is very delightful and gives immense happiness. Here, one is quite unconcerned with what may or may not result from one's actions; the work is done entirely for its own sake, for the love of it..... What alone is worthy to be called "action" is that action by which man's eternal union with God becomes revealed, all the rest is useless, unworthy of the name of action, not action at all......... Egoless work is full of beauty, for it is not promoted by a desire for self-gratification...........................

—Mata Amirtanandamayi

It is in the best interest of a man to become a karma-yogi and work to the best of his abilities and without bothering about results.

—Sam Veda

8. FREE WILL VIS-À-VIS DIVINE WILL

We often come across the question as to whether our lives are totally governed by fate? Can free will shape our lives? Which is stronger, fate or free will? Some sages say that we make our own destiny. Some declare that it is only the divine will that prevails.

The future is carved out of the present moment. Tomorrow's harvest depends upon today's ploughing and sowing. The past is dead and the future is not yet born. If one is inefficient and unhealthy in the present, he has no reason to hope for greater future... The action of today becomes the destiny of tomorrow. If, after all our efforts, the vasanas are not totally exhausted, then the balance that remains to trouble us is called 'destiny'. Man can change his destiny not by wishing for it, but by working for it.

—Swami Chinmayananda

The above uttering of Swami Chinmayananda is in support of free will. While *Koushitaki Upanishad* supports divine will, views in support of free will are found in *Brihadaranyako Upanishad* and in *Maitri Upanishad.* Let us see them now.

Whomsoever the Lord desires to lift upwards, by him He causes good deeds to be performed. Whomsoever He resolves to push down, by him He causes bad deeds to be performed.

—Chapter-III, Verse-9, Koushitaki Upanishad

Man is full of desires. His inclinations will be shaped by his desires. His deeds will be shaped by his inclinations. And he will reap the fruit suited to his deeds.

—Chapter-IV, Verses-4&5, Brihadaranyak Upanishad

You are what your deep driving desire is; As your deep driving desire is, so is your will; As your will is, so is your deed; As your deed is, so is your destiny.

—Maitri Upanishad

In *The Bhagavad Gita,* Lord Krishna, persuading *Arjuna* to fight the war and kill his foes, goes to the extent of saying as under:

By me they are already overcome. Be thou the outward cause,
dexterous one

—Chapter-XI, Verse-33, The Bhagavad Gita

Here, the prevalence of divine will is strongly supported.

The question as to whether it is free will or divine will that guides man's life remained the most difficult one to be answered. It still remains so and will continue to remain so as long as humanity exists on the earth. A great many sages have opined differently and a few have even accepted their inability to decide upon.

Sage *Arutprakasa Vallalar*, who is regarded as the foremost of the saints and sages of the nineteenth century, who is reported to have attained a deathless body and dematerialized his body to become one with the Almighty sings as under:

Read I, all the worldly knowledge through books-nay,
it is You Lord who made me learn;
Lost I, my interest in them, later in life-nay,
it is You Lord who made me loose interest;
Gripped I, firmly Your lotus feet as my rescue-nay,
it is You who made me grip your Lotus feet;
Acted then I, as if I got your grace at last;
Did I act myself, or is it You who made me act so?

When even a great sage like *Vallalar* stood perplexed at the mechanism of the interplay between free will and divine will, ordinary mortals can not come to a conclusion with ease. Hence, both the arguments prevail, viz., that of those who say that fate can be modified or overcome by free will and that of those who believe that it is all only divine will that prevails and man has nothing to do.

It is stated in *Yajnyavalkya Smriti* that success is achieved by both *daiva (purva karma)* and *purusha* acting in cooperation. God helps those who help themselves. What is required is sustained exertion in the proper direction. If it is maintained that God does everything and that man has no freedom in any matter, it would be shifting man's responsibility to God and finding an easy excuse for man's improper activities. Hence, the *Brahmasutras* declare that God distributes rewards strictly according to merits. This view points to the fact that there is scope for doing good deeds out of one's own free will.

Now let us consider the stand that there exists only the divine will. Those who believe that only the divine will prevails, sees free will only as an illusion. Though one may appear to be acting as per his free will discriminating between good and bad, it is only the divine will that exists in the background that makes one act the way he acts. In other words, there is no freedom to act. All acts are that of the divinity – good and bad, right and wrong, desirable and undesirable. It is like a puppet show. Human beings act according to the divine will just as the toys act according to the will of the puppeteer. If the toys think that they have their own free will, it is only an illusion. Does such a stand shake the very foundation of the *karma* theory? The answer is both yes and no. Yes, because one has no free will to choose his mode of action. No, because the effects of good and bad actions are not denied. So you reap as you sow. But it is the divine will that makes one sow a particular seed and reap its consequent fruits. The strength of this theory is that man becomes totally free the moment he realizes that there exists only the divine will and nothing else. When everything happens according to a divine plan, what am I to worry about? I am totally free. The very absence of free will gives enormous freedom to man and he gets relieved of all mental burden.

9. SUBMISSION TO THE DIVINE WILL

Though free will and divine will are discussed at length in many Hindu scriptures, it is the divine will that is given a prominent position. It is divine will that is considered to guide activities, including the free will.

It was God who vested every individual with the notion of free-will. Only when he is unable to execute what he wishes, would a person realize that a greater power is guiding him from within. So, if one submits to the divine will, there will be success. Saints are so attuned to God that whatever they think happens. Like a bubble in the river being swept in the direction of the current as it does not resist it, there will not be disappointments in life when man learns to surrender to God and ***accept*** *the outcome as His grace.* —*Swami Gautamananda*

When it is only the divine will that prevails, the secret of leading a peaceful, purposeful and contented life lies in submitting oneself to the divine will. Hence, surrendering to the divine will has been the essence of most of the Hindu religious scriptures. When one surrenders to the divine will, it helps him/her in two ways. First, he/she will lead a stress-free, happy and contented life on the earth, notwithstanding the adversities that he may have to face. Second, since he/she accepts life as it is, without anticipating anything and without complaining, he adds no further load to his *sanchita karma.* Some of the utterances of *Paramahansa Yogananda*, the Indian *yogi* who demonstrated to the world the effectiveness of *kriya yoga* throws light on the way of leading a life, submitting to the divine will.

Every morning I ask Him to tell me what He wants me to do; then I see Him work through my hands and brain and everything goes as He wishes. —*Paramahansa Yogananda*

I take on more and more work but I never feel I am overburdened, because I do everything for Him. I love Him and that surrender to God has destroyed in me the karma of ignorance.

—*Paramahansa Yogananda*

Even the most favoured person, one who appears to have everything, may not be happy. And you will never be satisfied for long with earthly things. They give only a false peace and contentment. The whole world has been plunged into chaos through greedy desires. Greed is creating war. Nothing else is causing it............

You should learn to be happy with what you have. Don't wish for anything more than what is already coming to you. ***The Father knows what you need****.* —*Paramahansa Yogananda*

Despite utmost personal effort and other deeds, that which is to be attained is attained by the individual only through Ishvara's Grace.

—*Section-6, Verse-38, Yoga Vasishta.*

Submission to the Divine will by a *Karma Yogi* has been brought out clearly by Aurobindo as under:

"...The path of work that karma yoga enjoins is an entire dedication to God. Every activity of life is offered as a sacred sacrifice to the Lord. ***The individual will is surrendered to the Supreme will at work in the cosmos.*** *The normal motive of ego-desire is to be renounced. This practice of eliminating the ego as the lever of operations of life-activities brings about a purification of the mind and will. Not only is activity undertaken without personal desire, but even the claims for the fruits of action are given up. Works are undertaken as they come without exercise of personal choice. Even the sense of individual doership is shed. The worker learns to feel the universal energy, the 'sakthi' of the Lord moving through his limbs. The whole life becomes a saga of self-dedication with no desire-motive to bind him to the wheels of 'samsara'. As he performs works without desire, without personal initiation, he is freed from the shackles of karma....."*

—*Sri Aurobindo*

No freedom has man to choose
On his birth and death;
Ridiculous it is thinking he is the
Doer of any act in between.

—*Yogi Vemmanna*

Subramania Bharathi, the great Tamil poet who exhibited the qualities of an enlightened soul sings beautifully as under as to how he lived a life surrendering to the divine will.

I surrender unto Thee, my Goddess
I surrender unto Thee.
Getting rid of the agony that accompanies my actions
And deriving satisfaction in doing Thy actions,
I surrender unto Thee.

—*Subramania Bharathi*

The sum and substance of Gita, according to my view is: Surrender oneself to God and completely efface the ego.

—Swami Turiyananda

The famous American philosopher Ralph Waldo Emerson (1803 – 1882 A.D.) sees as to how man gets into the web of destiny.

The efforts which we make to escape our destiny only serve to lead us into it. *—Emerson*

According to *Emerson*, the more we try to do things to escape from the claws of destiny, the more we fall into it. The great Tamil saint poetess Auvaiyar who lived in South India during the thirteenth century gives a gem of an advice as to how to overcome fate.

The only way to overcome fate
Is fixing up mind only on God;
All other acts will lead only to fate.

—Auvaiyar

Emerson leaves at saying that our own very efforts lead us to our destiny. While Auvaiyar points out that all our efforts leads only to our own fate (which *Emerson* had realized six centuries latter), Auvaiyar gives the tip to overcome this by submission to the Divine will by saying that one should act in this world by fixing mind only on God. Surrendering one's will to the Divine will relieves one from the burden of carrying the *karmic* load and thus relieves one from the claws of destiny.

Everything in the Universe abides in the Supreme Being. Realize this well; realizing this, cast off the desires that rise in the heart... joy comes only by giving up of desires and attachments.. You may live the longest life, doing work in a detached spirit and dedicating everything to God... Thus only can we escape the contamination of work and sterilize life.........

—Isavasyopa Upanishad

Life is but
A drama directed by God.
The script is already written; We
have but to wait and watch.
The law of life is: accept, accept
and accept ! It's all His will.
But this realization comes only
when our little wills are merged
in the larger Divine will.

—J.P.Vaswani

10. UNCONDITIONAL ACCEPTANCE OF LIFE, THE UNIQUENESS OF A GREAT LEADER

The quality of acceptance develops only when one submits to the Divine will. Acceptance is a great quality. When you accept something, you give it the freedom to be what it is; you don't want it to be different from what it is; you don't demand any change, any modification. How do you accept the sky? How do you accept the sea? You don't want the sky to be different. You don't want the sea to be different. This is because you have no control over them. You can't change the colour of the sky. You can't change the depth of the sea. The dancing waves of the sea won't listen to you if you ask them to calm down. So, you accept them as they are. You never complain that the sky is blue in colour. This is the frame of mind required for accepting anything and everything around.

If what I want
for myself is contrary to what
God wants for me, let me want
only what God wants and
I shall be at peace.

—*J.P. Vaswani*

One who has the quality of acceptance will accept his father, mother, brothers, sisters, friends, foes, relatives, neighbours, strangers, life-partner, colleagues, subordinates, superiors and every human being as they are. An organizational leader who has the quality of acceptance will accept all the members of the organization and all the stake holders, as they are. He will not expect them to be different, though he himself may have views that are opposite to others' views. The trouble arises only when one is not prepared to accept things as they are. Many find it difficult even to accept their past, leave alone accepting what happens at present. Past is something that has already happened. No one can change it. The past comprises of many characters, many situations, many turn of events–some painful and joyful.

Many people have played their part and each one has contributed his/her part. It is all gone now. The play is over. It can't be replayed. The play can't be expected to be different. If one does not accept the drama that has already been completed he/she will only retain pain and anger, blaming somebody or some incident for his/her misery. The quality of unconditional acceptance of the worldly activities will come only through submission to the Divine will.

O Lord, give me,
If not a cheerful frame of mind,
An objective frame of mind, so that
I can accept all characters
Who played roles in the drama of my life.
What a drama !
I do not want to change the drama;
It has already been staged.

—*Swami Dayananda Saraswathi*

Saint *Thayumanavar* puts forth the presence of Divine will in his own style as under:

Not even a smallest of particles moves
But for His wish.
Had this been known,
What is wisdom? What is foolishness?
Who is wise? Who is unwise?
Who is great? Who is mean?
Who is a friend? Who is a foe?
....
....
Anything and everything is only
As per His wish.

—*Saint Thayunamavar*

11. CONCLUSION

Even if one finds it difficult to accept that there exists a Divine-will that keeps the world functioning in the way it is, he/she can abstain from adding further *karmic* loan by resorting to the performance of *nishkama karma* for which he/she can use his free will. By performing *nishkama karma* one accepts whatever life brings. Life is not going to follow one's choices. One can not force life to be according to what one desires. It is better to flow with the river than swimming against the current and that will bring more contentment and happiness.

How does a leader stand to benefit by either accepting the divine will or by performing *nishkama* karma? In both the instances, the person is in total acceptance. When one accepts the divine will, he surrenders himself totally to the Almighty. He will be performing his activities in the world, but with a different state of mind. He will allow the divine designs to flow through him and will remain an instrument in the hands of God. He will accept everything that happens in life as a *prasada* of God. Graceful acceptance of whatever comes out of our effort, an effort that is free from any sort of attachment over the results, with reverence and a sense of thanks is called *prasada bhuddhi*. When the leader accepts free will and performs actions without attachment to their fruits, i.e., when he performs actions as *nishkama karma*, he will remain untouched, unencumbered by worldly activities and there will a profound stillness in him that he will be performing his actions accepting everything totally, without weighing their merits and demerits, their pros and cons. The sense of equanimity will prevail in such leaders and it will keep them at ease and will improve their effectiveness in handling crisis situations.

Suffering is inevitable for all embodied beings. In this respect, there is no difference between the wise and the ignorant. But, here lies the difference. The wise man endures affliction calmly whereas the ignorant man makes himself miserable by constantly weeping and wailing.

—Tulsidass

5

CHAPTER

Overcoming Stress, the Silent Killer

Joy and sorrow, the agreeable and the disagreeable continually revolve (as on a wheel) among living creatures. Relying upon such understanding, the man of intelligence and wisdom lives at ease.

—Bhishma

1. INTRODUCTION

With the growth of organization and technological development, mentally stressed personalities also grow in number. More and more mental ailments are reported than physical ailments. Psychologists confirm that most physical ailments have their origin at mental stress. Man's technical progress and the so called modernization have made him forget that he himself is a biological being. As Benjamin Franklin puts it, man has become a tool-making animal. The whole humanity is in a hurry. Nobody knows where they have come from and where they are going – no knowledge of the source and no knowledge of the destination; yet all are in a great hurry, making every effort to reach nowhere. In the road of life, all are in the middle of the road, not knowing the beginning and the destination. But every one is busy, hurrying through. It only creates mental stress. Though mental stress, as a recent phenomenon sweeps through the entire humanity, the worst affected are business men and business executives. Of the two, of late, the business executives are becoming more and more stressed since business expects a lot from them and they are under compulsion to perform a tight-rope-walking in a world where the jungle rule of "survival of the fittest" has become a golden rule of business. The result, any business executive worth the name is constantly under mental stress.

2. MENTAL STRESS, THE DISEASE OF THE MODERN AGE

Stress has become the major disease of the modern age. It is estimated that more than 75% of all medical complaints are stress-related. This estimate indicates the gravity of the situation and gives a caution for the immediate need to treat mental stress. Present day business executives are more stressed personalities than their counterparts of yester years. In every possibility, executives of the future are going to be more stressed personalities than the present day executives. The list of stress-related disorders is endless. Increase in blood pressure, insomnia, peptic ulcer, stomach disorders, back pain, neck pain, body ache, skin disorders, rapid and irregular heart beats, migraine, brain-fag, bronchitis, cysts, tooth decay, tooth cavities, obesity, paralysis, hair-loss, arthritis, diabetes, menstrual difficulties, joint-pains, etc... are found to be diseases that have mental stress as their root cause. Homeopathy, the emerging alternative for allopathic treatment of diseases, considers mind symptoms as the crucial category of symptoms for identifying the disorder that a patient suffers from. The famous repertory of the Homeopathic Materia Medica by Dr. J.T. Kent has more number of pages devoted to mind related symptoms than physical symptoms. Physiologists have found out that in response to stress, pituitary gland secretes a body chemical called Adrenocorticotropic Hormone (ACTH) into the blood which induces the adrenal gland to produce other body chemicals called adrenaline and norepinerphine. The release of these chemicals into the human body system gives rise to increase in blood pressure and increase in blood sugar level. A recent study at Ohio's State University has found evidence that short periods of psychological stress can cause the body to take longer to clear heart-damaging fats from the blood stream. Thus, the connection between mental stress and physical ailments has been established beyond doubt. *Yoga Vasishta* describes the relationship between mental malady and physical malady as under:

When the mind gets unsettled, the body gets into a malfunctioning condition... When disease sets in, the nerve-channels abandon their normal balance while carrying the 'prana' current. When the 'prana' flow becomes abnormal, the nerve channels get paralysed....... With the flow of prana in nerve channels getting paralysed, the food turns harmful........ wrong digestion, indigestion and excessive digestion result from the paralysis of the nerve channels. Thus it is, bodily malady arises from the mental malady.

—Section-6, Chapter-9,Verses 99-102, Yoga Vasishta

Apart from physical ailments, loss of memory, lack of concentration, disturbed sleep, restlessness, irritation, anger, depression, anxiety, absent-mindedness, impatience, misanthropy etc., are some of the mental/

emotional ailments that affect a stressed person directly. The scientific and technological advancements have, while on the one hand promised better physical comforts to man, on the other hand robbed him of his mental peace and consequently his physical well-being. The factors responsible for the creation of stress are called "stressors". Stressors arise due to demands of life. Of all the factors that act as stressors, disruption of normal home life like death, divorce, separation etc., have been found to be the major contributors. Angry boss, indifferent subordinates, ungrateful customers, clandestine competitors, unwanted visitors, unachievable targets etc., are some of the factors that may act as stressors for a business executive. As Shakespeare wrote, "Things are neither good nor bad, but thinking makes them so", the attitude of the individual is the key to proper stress management. The solution to the problem of stress management lies in changing the attitude of the individual rather than manipulating with the stressors. Stressors can not be eliminated as they originate from the environment. And changing the environment is not in one's hand. Hence, having the right attitude towards stressors is the only way to overcome their effect. As the physical, mental and emotional ailments due to stress will affect business executives, there is an imperative need for them to learn as to how to manage stress.

3. STRESS MANAGEMENT TECHNIQUES

Many techniques for stress management have been developed and many are being developed. The stress management techniques advocated fall into two major divisions, viz., that of relaxation techniques, physical exercises and psycho therapy that are recommended by the Westerners and that of Yoga, meditation and allied mind-stilling techniques that are popular in the East. India had reached the peak of spiritual wisdom long time back and many lofty spiritual thoughts have their origin in this country. Yoga is most widely acknowledged as a stress management technique. We hear about busy executives joining short term courses on Yoga in order to help them overcome the stress and strain of business life. We also come across those who advocate Yoga as a means of attaining good physical health by performing certain *asanas* (yogic postures). Yoga is considered more as a physical exercise aiming at good physical health which in turn is believed to improve mental health.

4. UNDERSTANDING YOGA, THE SCIENCE OF MIND

Patanjali Maharishi, the propounder of Yoga defines Yoga as "the process of stilling the mind". The objective of stilling the mind is to merge the individual soul (*Jivatma*) with the universal soul (*paramatma*). According to Patanjali Maharishi, Yoga is "*Citta vrtti nirodha*" which means stilling the vibrations of mind. It is the elimination of all thoughts and initiation into pure awareness. In his *Yoga Sutra*, Patanjali Maharishi talks more about dealing with the mind than about practising certain physical postures of the body. Let us contemplate on a few verses from the *Yoga Sutra* of Patanjali Maharishi in order to have the right understanding of the meaning of Yoga.

> *"Yoga is the cessation of mind; then the witness is established in itself; in the other states there is identification with the modifications of the mind."*
>
> —*Yoga Sutra*

According to Patanjali Maharishi, Yoga is the cessation of mind. It is a state of no-mind. Mind is an activity. It is not the brain. Brain is physical while mind is not so, just as stomach is physical while hunger is not physical. The words 'cessation of mind' covers all spheres of your mental activities, viz., all you know, all your desires, your hopes, your anticipations, your beliefs, your philosophies, your ethics, your values, your presumptions, your suppositions, your religious values, your feelings of happiness and sadness etc. In fact, it covers everything that you 'know'. Cessation of mind means cessation of the known. Patanjali Maharishi wants you to give up totally, whatever you know. In fact, when he says that Yoga is the cessation of mind, even the thought that you ought to give up (or you are giving up) all that you know should not be present. It is the total dropping of the mind that is expected. It is moving from the known to the unknown.

Whether you practise doing the yogic postures or *pranayama* is not the issue. You may be doing all the postures; you may be inhaling and exhaling your breath in a systematic way as taught by your master. But, if your mind has not dropped from you, you are not in Yoga. After defining Yoga as the cessation of mind, Patanjali Maharishi gives the technique of achieving the state of no-mind. He says *"Then, the witness is established in itself"*. Cessation of mind is not something that can be achieved easily. We have been carrying our mind for so long, maybe for so many births. Hence, it is highly difficult to comprehend the state of remaining without mind.

In the process of making the mind remain still, there is an imminent danger that the mind will creep in and remain very much active under the pretension of trying to see what happens when the mind stills down. J. Krishnamurthy cautions against this.

What lies beyond can be found only if the mind is still. There may be something or there may be nothing at all. So, the only thing that is important is for the mind to be still. Again, if you are concerned with what lies beyond, then you are not looking at what the state of actual stillness is. If stillness to you is only a door to that which lies beyond, then you are not concerned with that door, whereas what is important is the very door itself, the very stillness itself. Therefore, you can not ask what lies beyond. The only thing that is important is for the mind to be still.....

—J. Krishnamurthy

Now we understand that though it looked simple, stilling the mind is not that easy a task. It has eluded many for long. Patanjali Maharishi gives a technique – a simple technique. He asks you to remain a witness to your mind. When you are in deep sleep, your mind has ceased. But, you are not aware of it. You don't remain a witness to your deep sleep. When you remain a witness to your mind, you are not concerned with its activities. You are not bothered whether your mind exists or has dropped. Your every effort to drop your mind will become an obstacle for the process of dropping the mind. Let the mind do whatever it is doing. You simply remain a witness. You have no truck with your mind. You are only an onlooker. Thoughts may be passing through. It is not possible to expect that your mind will get dropped as you wish. It may cling to you very strongly. But, Patanjali Maharishi asks you not to be concerned with it. You neither resist your mind, nor cooperate with it, but just remain a witness. When there is no mind, you are established in your witnessing. When you have become a witness to the activities of your mind, you cease to be a doer. Except in the state of witnessing in all other states you are identified with the mind. When you get identified with the mind, you have missed. The goal of *yoga* is to achieve a state of no-mind, a thoughtless state. When one becomes thoughtless, he becomes egoless and remains simply being which opens up the mystery of life.

What Patanjali Maharishi had revealed has been the experience of many saints. Saint Thayumanavar (who lived in South India during the eighteenth century) speaks on the same lines of Patanjali Maharishi.

"Oh God! Give me the sacred mindless state,
without making me think, I, me and mine
and fall into the bondage of worldly life

....

I wish to just remain, day and night
without speaking and thinking, Oh, my Lord!

....

without scrutinizing the scriptures,

without engaging in thoughts,
without even striving to attain mindless state
just seeing AS IT IS, will bring forth joyfulness million fold.”

—Thayumanavar

5. YOGA VASISHTA, A BOOK OF IMMENSE VALUE

Among the spiritual literatures of India, the two epics that stand out and that have in them wealth of information on how life should be lived, are The Ramayana and The Mahabharata. Lord Rama, the hero of the epic The Ramayana is an example for man to emulate. He is personification of all lofty qualities like honesty, modesty, magnanimity, kindness, nobility, tranquility and truthfulness. A look into the life of Lord Rama reveals that he got transformed into a totally serene and enlightened personality after listening to the discourses of His guru, saint Vasishta. The Yoga Vasishta, also known as The Brihat (the great) Yoga Vasishta contains about 32000 *slokas*. It narrates the conversation between Lord Rama and Vasishta. It contains the discourses of Vasishta on the most essential knowledge that a human being should attain, the knowledge after attaining which nothing else remains unknown. It deals with the subject of effecting union of individual soul with the ‘Supreme Soul’.

Lord Rama faced the challenges before his life with an undisturbed, tranquil state of mind, following the path of *Dharma.* The teachings about life that Lord Rama obtained from Vasishta, his *guru*, stood him in good stead throughout his life. *Yoga Vasishta* contains wisdom of the highest order that only an enlightened soul can interpret and explain the meanings of the text contained in it. However, trying to understand certain instructions of Vasishta that are simple and straight forward in meaning and contemplating on these instructions will throw light on the way life should be lived in this material world. This will help one perform his duties with an undisturbed state of mind, to remain tranquil and stress-free despite being surrounded by multitude of problems.

It is the mind that is the root cause of pain and pleasure that one experiences. Vasishta’s teachings progressively lead the seeker to the conviction that the objective world does not exist and that is it only a creation of the mind. All the mental stresses that human beings undergo are due to false identification. But, it will be a very hard task to make one understand that the physical world that exists around is a creation of the mind. Hence, sage Vasishta goes step by step in making the reader at least get a glimpse of the unreality that prevails around.

It is the non-existent stream of water that appears to flow with waves in a mirage; it is through mind, the delusive panoramic world is fancied as existing.

—Section-3, Chapter-1, Verse-19, Yoga Vasishta

As the world seen around is said to exist only due to mind, Vasishta affirms that only through conquest of mind heavenly happiness is obtained.

Only through conquest of mind, supreme beatitude is attained.

—Section-3, Chapter-1, Verse-59, Yoga Vasishta

Material gains and worldly attainments are not capable of bringing mental peace to one. Mental peace descends once mind gets stilled.

Wealth saves not, friends and relations help not. Nor physical exercises like asanas or pilgrimage or fasts or holy waters help a man to attain goodness.

—Section-3, Chapter-1, Verse-59, Yoga Vasishta

It is only through its own fancy, mind becomes bound. When the mind becomes extinct, liberation certainly results.

—Section-3, Chapter-8, Verse-4, Yoga Vasishta

When the entire world seen around is said to be the creation of mind, mind can be destroyed by the process of negating the world around. Mind can not be destroyed by fighting with it or by controlling it.

'I am so and so', 'this is mine' – such imaginations alone constitute the mind. By the negation of such thoughts, the mind gets destroyed, as a tree is cut off by the saw.

—Section-3, Chapter-9, Verse-17, Yoga Vasishta

It is mind that is the creator of the world; mind is the real person. That what is done by the mind is considered as really done and not that which is done by the body.

—Section-3, Chapter-5, Verse-1, Yoga Vasishta

It is mind, through thought process binds man to the world and make him undergo the sufferings. One gets liberated when he becomes mind-free.

To indulge in sankalpa, thought is great bondage; not to indulge in sankalpa is liberation.

—Section-6, Chapter-16, Verse-107, Yoga Vasishta

Assuming that one succeeds in destroying his mind, the question arises as to whether one can continue to function in the world after destruction of mind. Though complete destruction of mind is most difficult and very rare to come by among ordinary mortals, the mere awareness about the futility of mind's creations will calm down the oscillations of mind and will make one free from the effects of pains and pleasures.

Sorrows, desires, afflictions get destroyed like darkness before sun, in the case of persons with calm mind.

—Section-2, Chapter-1, Verse-61, Yoga Vasishta

Thus, the first step in overcoming the oscillations of mind is to understand that whatever happens around are all merely creations of mind and are not real.

Sage Vasishta knows very well that religious scriptures are not meant for reading and preserving but are meant for practising and adhering to. Religious scriptures are not meant to make one shun life and retire to the forests, giving up worldly responsibilities. They are meant to make one understand what reality is and having understood the reality, still perform worldly activities with a sense of detachment, like drops of water rolling over lotus leaves. Such a person, who remains internally in union with the ultimate and still externally performs the worldly activities unattached, untouched is a *Jeevan mukta.* Though such a person performs many acts, he performs them only physically; mentally he stays apart. As such, he remains unaffected by the results of his action. When one stays mentally apart from whatever he is doing, he gets insulated against mental stress. Let us contemplate on some of the verses contained in Yoga Vasishta.

Know Rama, that which is done mentally is really done; that which is renounced mentally is really renounced.

—Section-2, Chapter-1, Verse-61, Yoga Vasishta

When a business executive is fortunate enough to have at least a shade of qualities of a *Jeevan mukta*, he will perform the worldly activities in a state of tranquility and will remain mentally untouched by the results of his actions and will get insulated against mental stress.

He, in whom all the restless worldly strivings have become stilled, he who though talented appears to be otherwise, he who though thoughtful, is without thought – such one is a Jeevan mukta.

—Section-3, Chapter-2, Verse-96, Yoga Vasishta

He who goes through all kinds of experiences, as though he is a mere onlooker and remains inwardly cool and whole, is a Jeevan mukta.

—Section-3, Chapter-2, Verse-97, Yoga Vasishta

On how a *Jeevan mukta* will perform the worldly duties, Vasishta quotes the example of king Janaka and quotes as under:

He does not anticipate the future nor grieves over the past. Attending to the present work on hand, he remains smiling.

—Section-5, Chapter-1, Verse-64, Yoga Vasishta

Quoting the example of king Janaka, Vasishta instructs Lord Rama as to how to perform worldly activities, which in fact can be taken as an advice that is given to the world at large and to the mentally stressed personalities in particular, revealing the secret behind stress-free living.

Internally renouncing all desires, attachments and vasanas, externally attending to all tasks, do sport in the world, O Rama.

—Section-5, Chapter-1, Verse-64, Yoga Vasishta

Vasishta discloses a great secret when he says that the world keeps functioning by the presence of the Supreme power. Whether the universe and the multitude of living beings are creations of the Almighty or they are merely part of existence which exist from time immemorial is a debate that can go on without reaching any sort of consensus. This is because of the fact that we try to measure the immeasurable. Mind, which is the tool that we use to get cognizance of such complex issues, is an inadequate tool. But, the regular, systematic and immaculate functioning of the universe following unwritten laws to perfection shows that there must be some force behind it. One may choose to call that force by whatever name which one prefers. Vasishta asserts that there exists the Supreme power behind the functioning of the world. (Let us see what David Ben-Gurion, Israel's first Prime Minister had to say: I once talked to Einstein. Even he, with his great formula about energy and mass agreed that there must be something behind energy !!!)

Even if the jewel wishes not, luster emanates from it; even so, in the mere presence of the Supreme, the world keeps functioning.

—Section-4, Chapter-5, Verse-3, Yoga Vasishta

When it is the Supreme power that does all the acts and not individuals you and me, then where is the need for worrying about anything at all ? Simply, you are a non-doer. If one understands that he is a non-doer (or at least if he realizes that the role played by him through his actions is just nothing when compared to the immensity of actions that happen across in the universe), he will remain untouched by the effects of performing worldly activities.

With the firm thought, 'I am a non-doer', in all condition, if a person keeps doing things that befall his lot, he is not tainted through the acts.

—Section-4, Chapter-5, Verse-6, Yoga Vasishta

6. MEDITATION, THE OTHER NAME FOR A STATE OF NO-MIND

Just like Yoga, the term meditation has also attracted the attention of busy and tense executives as a remedy for relieving mental stress. Meditation again has been grossly misunderstood. It is not concentration. It is a technique to attain a mindless state. Let us see what some great souls have said about meditation, which will coincide with the utterances of Patanjali Maharishi.

"Meditation is the freedom from thought .... meditation is not the mere control of body and thought, nor is it a system of breathing in and breathing out .... All effort to meditate is the denial of meditation."

—J. Krishnamurthy

"The excellence of mind is in abysmal stillness"

—Lao-Tzu

"Whirl around yourself and the word seems to whirl around you; stand till and everything is stilled within a vast stillness".

—Tukaram

"Stop ..... it is here; run ... it is nowhere".

—Hui-hai, a Zen master

"A mind which is occupied, with the thinking either of God or of Sex will not find peace and happiness."

—Swami Nirmalananda

"A meditative mind is silent. It is not the silence which thought can conceive of. It is the silence when thought – with all its images, its works and perceptions has entirely ceased."

—J. Krishnamurthy

Meditation is like entering into an unknown world of beauty and quietness; it is a world without image, symbol or word, without waves of memory. *—J. Krishnamurthy*

Meditation is freedom from thought and a moment in the ecstasy of Truth. *—Dr. S. Radhakrishnan*

Meditation means: drop all thoughts, drop all ideologies, drop knowledge, drop the mind itself. *—Osho*

The degree of the absence of thoughts is the measure of your progress towards self realization. *—Ramana Maharishi*

Though the languages of the different great men differ slightly, the message contained in them points to the same direction in that a mindless state is what is to be sought after. If one can attain a mindless state, he is in the state of Yoga, and this is the key for having a stress-free mind.

Even as fire without fuel finds peace in its resting place, when thoughts become silence, the soul finds peace in its own source.

—*Maitri Upanishad*

If you meditate with the motive that through meditation you will reach somewhere, achieve some goal, you are missing the point. Meditation can not have any motive. It is the process of dropping all motives.

7. CONCLUSION

The secret of the teaching of Lord Krishna, in the Bhagavad Gita – *'Do your duty, unmindful of the results'* can be best understood and practised only if one knows how to be 'unmindful'. This is a mental condition that Patanjali Maharishi recommends when he says *'Yoga is the cessation of mind'*. Only when one drops his mind by remaining a witness to whatever happens around, he could attain the 'unmindful' state. Once a person attains this state, he will remain stress-free however stressful the business environment may be in which he performs his duties. After all, greatest riddles in life have simple answers.

What is high? What is low?

These are but the inventions of man's vanity.

Let me cast aside the conceit of my self-intoxicated life.

Let me live a life without attachment to the fruits of action.

Lord, let me behold Thy beatific vision in every little thing of the world.

Lord, let me dedicate ally actions to Thee

—Thayumanavar

6 CHAPTER

Remaining Indifferent to the Core

Joy and sorrow, the agreeable and the disagreeable continually revolve (as on a wheel) among living creatures. Relying upon such an understanding, the man of intelligence and wisdom lives at ease

—Section CLXXIV, Santi parva, The Mahabharata

1. INTRODUCTION

The embracing situation that a leader quite often comes across is that he/she is required to assume responsibility for the shortcomings, inefficiency and incompetence of his/her team members. As any team consists of people of different calibres, it is more likely that there will be always some area where a team has not performed to the required level. This is in spite of the best efforts taken by the leader to mould the team and to guide the team towards the goal. How should a leader handle such situations? No doubt the leader has to find out as to where things really went wrong and should attempt to mend such weaker spots, be it systems or persons. Only then can the team improve upon its performance the next time. But, an effective leader will do the job without carrying any burden. He will be more active outwardly in accomplishing the task at hand but totally indifferent inwardly to what he is doing. A leader might come across many such situations where his position is threatened, his authority is questioned, his performance is under rated and his leadership is criticized. But a real leader will be indifferent to all such things. Looks anarchic? How can one be inwardly indifferent to what he is doing and still do his job better under such adverse situations? It may appear ironical but the secret behind effortless action lies here. By effortless action I mean a mind-set where the performer does not attach any importance to the outcome of his actions, where the performer just performs his part keeping himself mentally far away from his actions. In other words, he is indifferent to what he is doing. He attaches least importance to his actions, yet he acts efficiently, effectively, intelligently and acts much better than most other leaders who are considered best. Such indifference is a quality that is very rare to find. Because, people in general, are totally get them involved both physically and mentally in worldly activities. They have no time to stop for a while and to think as to what for all these activities are, as to why such hustle and bustle everywhere around.

Long identification with the material world has trained you that the false is true, that the temporary is eternal. You have to re-educate yourself into the right vision. —*Satya Sai Baba*

King Janaka, (father of Sita in the great Indian epic the Ramayana) was a great emperor. Yet he was a saint too. He is considered to be one of the enlightened souls. How can a saint, an enlightened person, still rule a country taking part in the day to day activities that will call for a greater involvement? Yes, Janaka ruled his country very effectively. He gave the best administration. Yet he was not attached to the worldly activities. Mentally he remained far apart from what he was doing physically. He was indifferent to the kingly role that he was performing. Contemporary business leaders can take a leaf from the treatise of king Janaka's life to learn the art of performing the worldly activities and yet remaining indifferent to the activities performed.

You are always engrossed in a war. Life is full of strife and turmoil. It is therefore in the best interest of one and all to take part in the war without desiring anything.

—*Verse 981, Sama Veda*

2. ASTAVAKRA GITA, A GREAT BOOK OF WISDOM

Astavakra Gita is a treatise on Advaita Vedanta. It is in the form of a dialogue between teenager sage Astavakra and his royal disciple king Janaka. It forms part of *vana parva* portion of the epic *The Mahabharata*. The teachings contained in Astavakra Gita are meant for a seasoned disciple – the disciple who is in an advanced state of self-realisation. The realization can dawn on him at any moment. He has to remove only certain final traces of ignorance left behind. Astavakra Gita helps such a person who is on the verge of attaining self-realisation to reach his destination. Hence, the meanings contained in the verses of Astavakra Gita are a little difficult to comprehend. One should have the acumen to read between the lines and comprehend the hidden meanings. For instance, the message contained in Astavakra Gita is that one should remain indifferent to the happenings around. It can be questioned as to how one can be successful in the world that calls for total involvement in one's job to maintain a competitive edge over other players in the field.

3. NEITHER THIS NOR THAT

Many religions of the east proclaim that desire is the root cause of all evils and that a person undergoes painful consequences only because of his desire towards some object, thing, position etc. Hence Gautama Buddha says, 'Give up desires'. Astavakra Gita also calls for giving up desires.

> *Who can be compared with a Liberated-one, who has no desires at all lingering in his heart, who is contented and totally indifferent to everything?*
> *—Astavakra Gita*

But, Astavakra Gita does not stop at advising to give up desires. It further goes on to say that the Liberated one is totally indifferent to 'everything'. He is not only indifferent to pleasure but also to pain. He is not only indifferent to success but also to failure. He is not only indifferent to his past actions but also to his future actions. He is neither concerned about birth nor about death. Such is the mental make-up of a Liberated-one. On the top of all, Astavakra Gita boldly declares that Liberated-one will be indifferent to even Liberation.

> *The Great-souled-one, who has realized the Truth, is free from desire for sense-enjoyments and for spiritual liberation.* *—Astavakra Gita*

> *As I have realized the Supreme Self who is the "Witness" and the Lord, I have become indifferent both to bondage and liberation; I feel no anxiety for my liberation.*
> *—Astavakra Gita*

King Janaka, the Liberated-one could rule his kingdom to perfection and yet could remain separated away from the influences of worldly activities, like a drop of water lying on lotus leaf. This was possible because he was indifferent to everything. Only such a person's mind will remain tranquil, still, motionless and serene. And a leader can acquire a tranquil mind only if he is indifferent to everything happening around just as king Janaka was. This is a quality most wanting, especially in the present day world, where every next person suffers from some kind of mental problem or the other. It is a quality very much required of a leader for him to become an effective leader.

Let us dwell a little further on the aspect of 'indifference to everything'. When a person is indifferent to everything, he will not carry the burden of the past nor will he develop anxiety about the future. This will keep him free from worries and anxieties. This will clear his mind of fears and anticipations.

The Liberated-one, who abides in the Self, under all conditions, is released from the idea of actions and of duty. He is the same everywhere, and due to the absence of desires in him, does not brood over what he has done and what he has not done. —*Astavakra Gita*

The indifference of a Liberated person is total. It is total renunciation. It is called *param vairagya* (Supreme Dispassion). It is total indifference, knowing fully well that all strivings are fruitless.

It is bondage when the mind desires or grieves at anything; does reject or accept anything; does feel happy or angry at anything.

—*Astavakra Gita*

The wise one is neither happy nor miserable,
neither attached nor unattached,
neither liberated nor an aspirant for liberation,
for he is neither this nor that.

—*Astavakra Gita*

All activities in the pursuit of desire, wealth and even *dharma* are all unreal. The very anxiety to attain liberation is an illusion; therefore it is said in *Astavakra Gita* that wise men will give up everything. It is a total renunciation. It is not controlling oneself from worldly activities. It is called *Param Vairagya* (Supreme Dispassion). It is total indifference, knowing fully well that all strivings are fruitless.

Where is the past? Where is the future?
Where, even, is the present? Where is space?
Where, even, is eternity for me
who abide in my grandeur?

—*Astavakra Gita*

Can it be possible for one who is indifferent to everything, to be an effective leader? This question remains very much to be answered. Astavakra Gita comes up with an answer.

He who has the ego-sense in him within, acts (Mentally), even though he does not act (Physically). Surely, the Wise-one, who is free from the sense of ego, does not act (Mentally), even though he acts (Physically).

—*Astavakra Gita*

A person who remains in-different does nothing 'mentally', though he will be very active physically. He will be bubbling with energy. He will be more effective than most of those who are attached to the worldly activities.

He, who transcends existence and non-existence, who is wise, contented, free from desires, does nothing, even if he be acting vigorously in the eyes of the world. —*Astavakra Gita*

He whose work has dropped off with the dawn of wisdom, gets no occasion to do or to say anything even though in the eyes of the ordinary people he is doing work. —*Astavakra Gita*

Despite being very active performing his duties, the Liberated-one will never get perturbed because he is fully aware that the whole universe that we come across, that we experience from birth to death is a product of illusion – an illusion created by the deceptive mind.

The Pure-one knows with certitude that this universe is the product of illusion and that nothing really exists. The Imperceptible Self is revealed to him and he, naturally, becomes tranquil. —*Astavakra Gita*

The fool, even in 'inaction' is ever agitated by his commotion within. But the adept (wise) even when performing duties, indeed, is unperturbed.

—*Astavakra Gita*

4. MEDITATIONLESS MEDITATION

As seen earlier, Astavakra Gita is a treatise that is meant for those who are on the verge of getting liberated. It gives a gentle push to the aspirant to jump out of the boundary of worldly affairs. Many Indian scriptures require an aspirant who is in search of the Truth to be in meditation. To become meditative is to become thought-free. Yet, there is a subtle element of fear here. One who is in meditation is still on the verge. He is yet to cross the boundary.

Completely give up even contemplation and hold nothing in your mind. You are indeed the Self, ever-free. What will you do by meditation?

—*Astavakra Gita*

Since a Liberated-one will be indifferent to everything, he will be indifferent to meditation as well. No doubt he will be in meditation in the sense that he will be thought-free. But, he will be indifferent to even thoughtlessness. He will be in meditation, not by striving to be in meditation, but by giving up meditation. Then, his indifference is total, to the core.

To give up meditation through meditation is the highest meditation. There is no greater meditation than the meditationless-meditation.

—*Chinmayananda*

"Meditation", to a man of perfection, whose mind is at rest, is a wasteful exertion. —*Chinmayananda*

Swamy Chinmayananda explains the subtle difference between meditation and meditationless meditation by the analogy of the relationship between sleep and sleeper.

To one who has slept, there can be no more any "attempt to sleep". To the sleeper there is no more anxiety to sleep; he is already asleep.

—*Chinmayananda*

5. ACTIONLESS ACTION

A realized person will be active in the sense of the world. But he will be totally inactive inside. This is what The Bhagavad Gita calls as 'action in inaction'.

He who can see inaction in action and action in inaction is the wisest among men. He is a saint even though he still acts.

—*Verse 18, Chapter 4, The Bhagavad Gita*

Such a quality in a person will make him a great leader. King Janaka was an enlightened ruler. He continued to be active in the world even after attaining perfection. Gita does not advocate avoiding or giving up action. It is not possible for one to remain actionless in the world. Let us see what Gita says on this.

King Janaka and others attained perfection through action alone. Even for the sake of enlightening the world, it is your duty.

—*Verse 20, Chapter 3, The Bhagavad Gita*

Such a person who performs action unmindful of the results, unattached to the actions or their consequences will perform his action as a child's play.

When a child is at play, we can not call it a 'work' though the child expresses its intelligence and exhausts its energy. It has nothing to gain by the play, nor will the child lose anything by not playing. Its play is but a natural explosion of its energy. Thus works the liberated person. There is no impulse of desire behind any of his activities.

—*Swami Chinmayananda*

'Do your duty, unmindful of the results' which is the essence of the message to humanity contained in the *Bhagavad Gita* can be practiced by one, only if he is indifferent to everything.

6. INDIFFERENT PERSON, THE BLESSED-ONE

The teenager sage Astavakra informs his royal disciple king Janaka as under:

Rare indeed, my son, is that blessed person whose passion for living, desire to enjoy and hunger to learn and know have been extinguished by observing the ways of men. —*Astavakra Gita*

The world around gives the richest experience for anybody. This experience that one gains is first-hand and no amount of learning can be a substitute to it. Even a casual observation will reveal the purposeless life lived by people in selfish passions, in fruitless tragedies and in barren sorrows. This is happening everywhere around everyone, all the time, openly, for anyone to see. Yet, people have become so numb that these happenings around do not create any influence on them. People take things for granted and pursue their life without carrying any meaning for their life. They partake in all its tragedies, sorrows and sufferings. Only a careful observer will be able to realize the futility of all things happening around. Astavakra calls such a person as the blessed one. Such a blessed person will be totally indifferent in his approach towards life. He will not pick and choose. He will have no desire to enjoy. Astavakra touches the essence of the issue when he says that such a blessed person will not even have any desire to learn and know. This is the highest state of indifference, the highest form of detachment. Even a passion to know will create attachment. He will then get attached to learning the scriptures, learning the Vedas, the Upanishads; he will be in search of *Gurus* in his yearning to know the ultimate truth. According to Astavakra, the blessed is the one who has even become indifferent to knowing the ultimate truth. But, majority of people are intellectually blind and deaf and hence they are not able to comprehend the futility of world around.

With desire dead,
Thoughts destroyed,
Indifference to the world,
He who needs nothing
Is the king of kings.

—*Kabir*

A question arises here as to why majority of people get caught in the web of worldly happenings, despite their coming across everyday the meaningless struggle that people go through in their life. And the other question is as to how to keep oneself 'away' from worldly affairs, yet functioning in this world and partaking in all its activities. There is an important thing to be noted here. When Astavakra says that the blessed one will be devoid of passion for living, desire for enjoying etc., it may appear to be a difficult proposition. Indeed it is. That is why we come across only people who get involved in worldly affairs, physically, mentally and intellectually. We very rarely come across a person who according to Astavakra is a blessed one. If so, does the path to becoming a blessed one that difficult? Astavakra gives the answer.

Finding nothing as acceptable and nothing as rejectable and having neither joy nor sorrow, 'O Brahman', thus do I, therefore, abide in Myself.

....

Observing again and again, the fluctuations of the forms of pleasures (and pains) etc., in-different circumstances, I have renounced good and evil, and I live in true happiness.

—*Astavakra Gita*

The above verses of Astavakra tell the simplest yet the most important truth. One can become indifferent by neither accepting nor rejecting anything. When it is said that such a person will be indifferent to enjoy the pleasures of the world, it is possible only if he is also indifferent to undergoing the pains. One can be indifferent to life only if he is equally indifferent to death. He neither accepts anything, nor rejects anything. He remains. That is the state of true indifference. Such a person will function in the world and take part in the worldly activities. He will be, in fact, more actively engaged; he will be more efficient. Yet he will be mentally away from such activities totally. He will not be attached to the world, but he will be totally detached. If a leader possesses this attribute of detached attachment, he will be very active physically, mentally and intellectually, contributing his maximum to the organization, but at the same time will remain totally indifferent to the results of his actions.

7. GIVING UP EGO

Let us now come to the crux of the issue. Saint Astavakra has explained many aspects of a liberated person. We are given to understand that such a person will be totally indifferent to everything. And we have seen what 'total indifference' refers to. In a way, it is indifference to even becoming indifferent. So far, so good. How to inculcate the habit of total indifference in a person? Astavakra says that by observing the futility of happenings in the world around, one can become indifferent. But, that is a very difficult proposition. No doubt every one is coming across the futility of worldly endeavours in their life time quite frequently. Still most of the people remain attached to the world. They don't participate in worldly affairs with a sense of detachment. This is how the world is. We have to accept the reality.

In The Mahabharata we come across a conversation between *Yudhishthira* and a *yaksha*. *Yudhishthira* answers the questions posed by the *yaksha*. It is worth contemplating this here.

Q: *Abandoning what, man becomes universally loved?*

A: Pride.

Q: *The loss of what yields joy?*

A: Anger.

Q: *Renouncing what man becomes rich?*

A: Desire.

Q: *Which is the best gain?*

A: Health.

Q: *What is tranquility?*

A: Contentment.

Q: *Who creates hell and heaven?*

A: Mind.

Q: *What is the origin of grief?*

A: Ignorance.

Q: *What loss cannot be compensated?*

A: Ill-spent time.

Q: *What is the wonder of wonders?*

A: Countless lives are dying constantly. Still the living man thinks that he will live for ever. This is the wonder of wonders.

Yes, In spite of coming across uncertainty every time, in spite of witnessing the futility of worldly endeavours every now and then, in spite of coming into contact with the death of kith and kin, in spite of knowing fully well that death robs one of everything and that it comes all of a sudden, man still lives in his own world of imagination. He imagines that death is for others and not for him and hence strives to achieve many things in his life time. This false identity drives man to be greedy, to be selfish, to get involved in the worldly affairs and suffer. Man can not be indifferent to anything till such time he knows that he is only a very, very tiny particle in the universe and that he can neither do nor undo things. Man will become indifferent only when the wisdom dawns on him that all things are done through him and that he does not really do things. But, it will not be as easy as it looks like. Man's ego will resist any thing that belittles him, that makes him look powerless. Hence, the struggle to conquer the world goes on and it will go on. Though Yudhishthira wonders at the attitude of man, man has not changed. Even today this remains the greatest of wonders. The reason is that man thinks that he is the 'doer' while he really is not. Astavakra comes out with an answer as to how one can become indifferent.

You, who have been bitten by the great black-serpent of egoism "I am the doer", please drink the nectar of faith, "I am not the doer", and be happy.

—Astavakra Gita

It is by giving up the 'I am the doer' belief that one can become indifferent to the core. Only by giving up ego, by surrendering before the will of omniscient, omnipresent Almighty one can come out of the clutches of likes and dislikes, good and bad, right and wrong, pleasure and pain. And he will become indifferent to the core because now he will allow himself to be carried away by the all pervading universal power.

8. CONCLUSION

A leader has to be very active, free from prejudices and unbiased in taking decisions. He should not get irritated at the simplest provocation. He should be perfectly balanced in his approach towards solving problems. He should have a still mind that does not carry any burden of the past or the future. He should be receptive to all ideas and opinions. This is possible only if the leader is one who finds action in inaction and inaction in action. Since such a leader will find inaction in action, he will perform his duties without any concern about the results.

Do your duty, unmindful of the results

—The Bhagavad Gita

A leader can deal with worldly possessions. But, he should not get attached to them. He should handle worldly possessions, considering himself to be a trustee. The words of Swami Chinmayananda aptly depict this point.

There is no harm if we possess things of the world, but it would be tragedy if the things of the world possess us. For example, if we possess wealth, we are free to be rich, but when the wealth possesses us, we become a slave to our own wealth.

—Swami Chinmayananda

The leader can take part in all worldly activities, but keeping a distance between 'him' and 'what he is doing'.

One should try to stay in this world like a lotus in the flower. Because if one remains attached to the worldly pleasures, one may not get away from their allurement..................So, one should stay indifferently in the world while constantly keeping one's attention riveted to Lord Vishnu.

—Chapter-5, Garuda Purana

(Keeping one's attention riveted to Lord Vishnu can be interpreted as keeping one's focus on attaining self realisation.)

An effective leader will be one who is contentment personified. He will remain calm deep down. His calmness will be so deep that nothing can create any disturbance.

Look within.
Be still.

—The Dhammapada

Like a broken gong
Be still and silent.
Know the stillness of freedom
Where there is no more striving.

—The Dhammapada

But, for one to attain such a state of mind as enumerated above, one has to be a person who is indifferent to everything happening around. He should be indifferent to the core. When indifferent to the core, the leader is better placed to discharge his organizational role to perfection and at the same time reach greater strides in his journey towards self realization.

Of what avail this restless, hurrying activity?
This heavy weight of earthly duties?
God's purposes stand firm,
And thou, His little one
Needest one thing alone;
Trust in His power and will
To meet thy need.
Thy burden resteth safe on Him
And thou, His little one,
Mayst play securely at His side
This is the sum and substance of all.

—Tukaram

7 CHAPTER The Joy of Self-actualisation

Among thousands of men, one perhaps strives for perfection; and among those who strive, one perhaps knows Me in My pure essence.
—Lord Krishna in The Bhagavad Gita

1. INTRODUCTION

Abraham Maslow's Heed-hierarchy theory places self-actualisation need at the top of hierarchy of needs. Self-actualisation need is a desire to achieve worthwhile accomplishment and to become what one is capable of becoming. The definition of 'self-actualisation' has been wrongly understood, as achieving the highest possible status that one is capable of achieving and performing the highest possible feat that one is capable of performing. If this were so, we would have come across many 'fully-satisfied' personalities among the Chief Executives, Executive Directors and General Managers of reputed organizations and among successful personalities in other walks of life like business, politics, professional practices etc. But, the reality is something different. Such persons like Chief Executives, Executive Directors, General Managers and so on who are at the top levels of organizational hierarchy and whose lower order needs have been satisfied are found to vent their views more or less in the same tone as the junior employees and employees in the lower/lowest cadres and the difference, if at all there is any, lies only in the language and the mode of expression. Thus, achieving self-actualisation remains a far cry. Either Maslow must be wrong or our understanding Maslow must be incorrect.

2. A SELF-ACTUALISED PERSON

Maslow has offered suggestions for people who wish to work toward self-actualisation. By examining the characteristics of self-actualised persons as depicted by Maslow, we can understand that self-actualisation is not a mere extension of the hierarchy of needs of the lower order, but it is a total transformation of human personality, making one to reach higher planes of living. Many great personalities in the Indian history have lived the Indian way of life in their bone and marrow and their lives stand as living examples of what a human being can become. *Mahakavi* (meaning, 'Great Poet') Subramania Bharathi is one such great personalities who lived on this earth, a life worth emulating. When Maslow said that it is a desire to become what one is capable of becoming, he would have certainly meant a total transformation of personality and not merely acquiring social status and performing enviable tasks. This will be evident when one goes through the characteristics that are attributed to self-actualised personalities. A comparison of the characteristics listed by Mallow of a self-actualised person with the life of Subramania Bharathi as revealed in his poems, offer an interesting study and one can get a glimpse of how a self-actualised person will be. In the following pages let us go through what Maslow has said of self-actualised persons and how Subramania Bharathi proves himself to be one.

(a) Identifies with the humankind as a whole

Maslow defines a self-actualised person as one who identifies himself with the humanity as a whole. Bharathi views the entire humanity as his brothers and sisters. His heart pains on seeing disparity among human beings and the strong among the humanity exploiting the weak. On seeing those who suffer without food, his heart gets moved and he asks the world to take a pledge to provide food for all and he even goes to the extent of condemning that the world be destroyed, even if a single individual suffers due to want of food.

Brothers and sisters are
the human beings on this earth;
How then, can the strong
exploit the weak and live ?

....

....

....

Let's destroy the entire world
if the world can't prove food for all
and keep even one starving.

—*Subramania Bharathi*

(b) Possesses unhostile sense of humour; can laugh at human condition, not at a particular individual

According to Maslow, the self-realised person will have a sense of humour that is unhostile towards any particular individual. But, he will laugh at seeing the condition of humanity as a whole.

Bharathi gets dejected on seeing the vices that has pervaded the human race. On the other hand, he observes birds living a happy, serene, blissful life. In one of his poems, he asks a bird as to how it could live so happily and in the words of the bird that comes out as its reply, Bharathi laughs at the vices that prevail only in human society and not among other living beings. Let us see how the bird replies:

Listen, my dear man,
none is great and none small
in our class;
None is poor and none accumulates wealth
in our group;
None is above and none is below;
And we all live with dignity.
Listen too, my dear man,
no theft, no treachery,
no ego, no petty knavery
in our breed.
All such mocking qualities belong to only thy race.

—*Subramania Bharathi*

In the words of the bird, Bharathi laughs at human conditions and wants men to learn the lesson on leading a happy life from the birds.

(c) Spontaneous and natural, particularly in thoughts and emotions

According to Maslow, since a self-actualised person has a free mind, free from inhibitions of all kinds, he will be spontaneous in his reactions to the situations that he comes across. He will neither hide his feelings nor modify his views due to compulsions. He will appreciate anything that is in tune with nature and will condemn anything that is against nature and justice. When Bharathi lived, it was a time at which quarrel between the fellow human beings was at its peak on the basis of caste and creed. Though many great works of seers and saints appeared and adorned the Indian literature, there also emerged derogatory views from the mean among the so-called literate people that also somehow entered the contents of religious and moral literatures. Bharathi stoutly opposed discriminating people on the basis of caste, creed and religion and did not fail to raise his voice against such discriminations. Bharathi's spontaneous outburst appears as below:

A code of conduct specifying
one code for the sudharas

and a different one for the bhramins
can only be a code of conspricy.
And not a code of conduct.

—*Subramania Bharathi*

(d) Capable of continued freshness of appreciation of even the simplest, the most common place experiences (for example witnessing a sunset, a flower etc.)

Maslow's self-actualised person knows how to appreciate even the simplest things in life. In fact, in what appears to be simple and trivial for others, the self-actualised person finds enough stuff to enjoy and appreciate. Bharathi was a great admirer of nature. In his poems, we frequently come across Bharathi praising nature and getting excited on coming into contact with nature and we find him sing in praise of things like the rain, the sun, the moon, the stars, the dawn, the dusk, the flowers, the birds, the bees, the trees, the woods etc. For him, these are not inert or insignificant objects. They are his kith and kin.

Crows and birds belong to our breed;
The bluish seas and the mountains, to our family.

—*Subramania Bharathi*

Bharathi observes a bull pulling a cart and moving along the road-side. He wonders as to how a cart could move which people consider as an inert object. The bull has life and its life gives the bull movement. If there is no life, there can be no movement. When the bull pulls the cart, the cart also moves along with the bull. Bharathi gets fascinated at such a sight which may look very ordinary in the eyes of the world. He, however, gets astonished and asks if the cart has also acquired life since it moves. Looks like a child's fantasy. But, that is how great souls live. And that is why Maslow has said that a self-actualised person will appreciate the most common place experiences and will derive freshness.

The cart moves, being pulled by the bull;
The bull has life;
Oh, the cart too has acquired life!
How else, can the cart move and move
like a living being.

—*Subramania Bharathi*

(e) Experiences mystic and oceanic feelings in which one feels out of time and place and one with nature

Maslow's self-actualised person will not be bound by time and space. In one of his poems. Bharathi identified himself not as an individual human being, but as everything that he sees around and thus moves out of time and space.

I am the birds that fly in the sky,
The animal that live on the land,
The trees that grow in the woods.
And I am the wind, the streams and the seas too.
I am the stars that twinkle in the skies,
The expanse of the space around,
The worms that crawl on the earth
And I am the creatures that live in the water too.

—*Subramania Bharathi*

(f) Thoughtful and philosophical

A self-actualised person will be thoughtful and at the same time philosophical, according to Maslow. Hindu philosophy speaks more about one word called '*Maya*'. It means illusion. According to the Hindu philosophy, the world that we see around is purely an illusion.

Like visions in a dream, so must we regard all things.

—*Sage Nagarjuna*

It is *Maya* that deludes living entities into forgetfulness of their spiritual nature and God. Man, who is under the influence of *Maya*, considers this world as real and suffers in ignorance. This is the essence of the Vedas, the Upanishads and other Hindu religious scriptures. Bharathi sees the illusionary world around and sings as under:

O ! Standing entities, walking beings and flying birds,
Are you all a dream?
Or misunderstood forms?
Learning, listening and thinking –
Are all these illusions, petty and meaningless?
O ! the skies, the sunlight and the abundance of trees,
Are you all a mirage?
The past has perished and been interred like a dream.
Am I too, a dream
And the world around, a falsehood?

—*Subramania Bharathi*

(g) Capable of some detachment from the culture in which one lives, recognizing the necessity for change and improvement

Bharathi sees with displeasure some of the ills in the culture of the people of his times. He welcomes change for good and wishes for a change in their attitude.

Ye, who speak in praise of
hundreds and hundreds of scriptures,
follow never in your deeds;
Those that speak about the Truth-
Ye, get away, get away.
Ye, who speak of
hundreds and hundreds of castes and creeds,
follow never the path of righteousness.
Ye, get away, get away.
Ye, who speak of
hundreds and hundreds of morals,
salute the immorality
when bribed with money,
Ye, get away, get away.
Ye, who will accept
Scriptures that speak about the Truth
as Vedas and abide by,
I welcome thee, welcome thee.
Ye, who will be scared
to speak the untruth
and will cast aside writings
containing falsehood,
I welcome thee, welcome thee.

—*Subramania Bharathi*

3. CONCLUSION

Out of the five needs that Maslow identified, the first four (physiological, safety, love and esteem needs) are mundane in nature and pertain to worldly activities. Self-actualisation need is one that exists in a different plane. If one does not possess or has not acquired the qualities required of a self-actualised person, he will never find satisfaction in spite of having all the comforts in life that one can think of. Self-actualisation need is a need is not one that can be satisfied by accomplishing something great.

It has been understood wrongly so. In has been misunderstood as an extension of the four lower order needs. The words of Albert Einstein are worth noting here.

Try not to become a man of success but rather to become a man of value.
—*Albert Einstein*

Being a self-actualisation person requires a total transformation of personality. It is a transformation from selfish to selfless attitude. It is a transformation from being an isolated individual to being one belonging to the entire world. Here again, the words of the genius Albert Einstein comes in support.

Only a life lived for others is a life worth while.
—*Albert Einstein*

In short, it is a transformation from an ordinary person to a real human being. It is becoming an unpolluted, unconditioned, free, fresh personality, rejoicing at the endowments that life has showered upon. Bharathi, though lived in poverty, possessed qualities of a self-actualised person visualized by Maslow, which fact leads to the inference that satisfaction of lower order needs is not a pre-requisite for one to become a self-actualised person. This is because, self-actualisation is transformation of one's personality from the mundane to the spiritual plane (or call it a higher order plane.)

The life of Bharathi, as evidenced from his poems, stands as adequate proof that he lived his life as a self-actualised person as visualized by Maslow and his way of life provides a pointer to those who opt to attain that stage.

Generations to come, it may be, will scarce believe that one such as this ever in flesh and blood walked upon this earth...............

We must all be happy and grateful that destiny gifted us with such an enlightened contemporary, a role model for the generations to come.....

—Albert Einstein on Mahatma Gandhi

8 CHAPTER

Truth Alone Triumphs

Live as if you were to die tomorrow. Learn as if you were to live forever.

—Mahatma Gandhi

1. INTRODUCTION

A study of Indian value system will not be complete without touching upon the life and teachings of Mahatma Gandhi. Mohandas Karamchand Gandhi (1869–1948) is a great human being who spent his life for the selfless service of the people of India. Refusing earthly possessions, he lived a simple but great life, sacrificing everything for the cause of the nation. He lived a spiritual and ascetic life amidst fighting for the freedom of India from the British rule. Indians revered him as a saint and started to call him 'Mahatma' Gandhi. The Sanskrit word 'Mahatma' stands for 'Great Soul' and Gandhi is really one of the rarest of rare personalities. Contemporary business leaders can take a leaf out of the volumes of ethical and moral instructions given by Gandhi through his lectures, books and more importantly through his own way of living and make use of the messages contained in them to improve their leadership skills. Gandhi is a great leader and he led the entire nation of India in its fight against the British rule for attaining freedom. He could do this mammoth task since he had his faith strongly rooted in spirituality and had firm belief on the influence of God in every human endeavour. Gandhi's deeply held spiritual beliefs were not exclusively Hindu. He quite often acknowledged his indebtedness to Christ's Sermon on the Mount, to the writings of Leo Tolstoy and Thoreau and the teachings of Zoroaster, Mohammed and Buddha, apart from The Bhagavad Gita, the Vedas and the Upanishads, which were his intimate companions in conducting the journey of life.

2. THE GIST OF GANDHIAN PHILOSOPHY

The philosophy advocated by Gandhi can be better understood if we look at what according to him, constitute sin. According to Gandhi, the following are the seven sins in this world.

- Wealth without work.
- Pleasure without conscience.
- Knowledge without character.
- Commerce without morality.
- Science without humanity.
- Worship without sacrifice.
- Politics without principle.

The above principles will help the corporate leaders a lot. Shareholder wealth improvement is no doubt the prime motive of any joint stock company. But a true leader, (being a true human being) will not attempt to improve shareholder wealth at any cost. He will do so only by fair means and not by foul means. He will not compromise for any short-cut method that lacks ethical values to earn wealth.

Character counts more than knowledge. Values count more than skills. A successful leader will give importance to character and moral values. He himself will adhere to certain ethical standards. He will see to it that no one who lacks ethical and moral values will form part of his team. A successful leader will always follow fair-practice. Though he will be aiming for improving the bottom-line of his organization, he will not conduct his trade without morality and will always stick to best trade practices at any cost. Obviously, this will stand him in good stead in the long-run.

Gandhi's view that science without humanity is a sin carries in it the value and importance he assigns to humanity. Gandhi attaches greater importance to welfare of mankind and shuns any development in the name of science and technology that is against human welfare. Conscious leaders can not ignore Gandhi's view for sure. After all, it is people who support any organization. Any organization exits to satisfy needs of the people and hence can sustain only if it has the continued support of people. Hence, it is obligatory on the part of organizations that they don't do or support any cause that is against the interests of people at large.

Though Gandhi was born Hindu, he embraced the views of many religions. He says that he regards Jesus as a great teacher of humanity. He was impressed by the personal and social codes of behaviour that Islam prescribes. Though he was influenced by The Bhagavad Gita, the holy book of the Hindus, he equally kept close religious scriptures of other religions.

According to Gandhi, religion is a matter of the heart. It is not external observance. It is faith in God and living in the presence of God. According to him, God is nothing but Truth. He affirms that he worships God as Truth only. According to Gandhi, religion and morality are inseparably bound with each other. To Gandhi, "There is no religion higher than truth and righteousness." When Gandhi says that worship without sacrifice is a sin, he goes to the peak of selfless service. When one worships God asking for what he does not have, he should be prepared to give what he has to those who ask for. Only when a person is ready to offer what he has to others, he qualifies to put forth his request to God asking for things that he does not have. This simple logic is revealed by Gandhi in crystal clear terms when he says that worship without sacrifice is a sin.

The sacrifice which causes sorrow to the doer of the sacrifice is no sacrifice. Real sacrifice lightens the mind of the doer and gives him a sense of peace and joy.

—Mahatma Gandhi

Those who don leadership roles will come across many situations that call for great scarifies on their part for the benefit of their followers. Leaders can sacrifice willingly only if they can taste the joy in it. And that requires a great understanding of life, its meanings, its purpose and its beauty. Sacrifice is the very order of nature. If a seed does not sacrifice, a plant can not come out. We are here in this world only because of the sacrifices done by so many people, so many other living beings, so many plants and trees. But, we are unaware of all this. The moment a clear understanding of these dawns on us, sacrifice will become a matter of joy. Then, we can look forward to sacrifice as an opportunity to repay our debt to the whole existence. It was such a mind-set that made Gandhi to sacrifice his life willingly, voluntarily to the cause of his nation and its people.

When politics without principle is considered as a sin, business without principle is a sin as well. A successful business leader will conduct his business on sound ethical principles. He will be respectful to all. He will treat others, be it employees, customers or competitors, with utmost respect. He will meet obligations to employees and customers regardless of the circumstances. He will pay high regards to honesty and integrity. And above all, he himself will abide by the ethical principles that he sets in.

3. VALUES GANDHI CHERISHED MOST AND THEIR RELEVANCE TO LEADERS

Some of the values that Gandhi cherished most in his journey of life and stick to them steadfast till the end will expose to readers, the secret behind Gandhi's successful life. Though it requires an indomitable spirit to tread the path of Gandhi, at least getting some glimpses of these values that Gandhi cherished most will clear our narrow vision of life and throw open before us the limitless opportunities that are available to us to make our life worth its name. Let us now dwell upon some of these values.

Truth

The word 'Truth' has its equivalent in Sanskrit and it is the word 'Satya'. The word 'Satya' is derived from 'Sat' which means 'being'. So, 'Truth' is that which exists. Nothing exists in reality except Truth. Hence, Gandhi quotes, "It is more correct to say that Truth is God than to say that God is Truth." Gandhi worshiped God as Truth. He was prepared to sacrifice the things dearest to him in his pursuit of his quest for Truth. 'Even if the sacrifice demanded be my life, I hope I may be prepared to give it', says Gandhi and his words were proved correct when he was killed by his very own countryman.

His relentless search for Truth made him a unique personality. The great hardships that he underwent, without worrying unduly about them were made possible because of his stern pursuit after Truth. His single minded devotion to Truth made him become indifferent to the dualities of life. This has made him acquire many noble qualities.

In the march towards Truth, anger, hatred, selfishness etc., naturally give way, for otherwise Truth will be impossible to attain. A man who is swayed by passions may have good enough intentions, may be truthful in word, but he will never find the Truth. A successful search for Truth means complete deliverance from the dual throng such as of love and hate, happiness and misery.

—Mahatma Gandhi

Thus, we could arrive at the obvious conclusion that what Mahatma Gandhi considered as Truth is nothing but what we, in common, consider as God, Almighty, Superpower, the omnipresent and omnipotent force etc. Instead of searching for God, Gandhi searched for Truth. Though he was impressed by Lord Rama and his ideal qualities, he is clear in his vision that his aim of life is to realize Truth. He did not allow religious prejudices to come in his way. According to him his God is Truth and his religion is Truthfulness. Gandhi is an ardent reader of religious literatures of all religions. The conclusion that he arrived at is that all religions of the world, while they may differ in other aspects, uniformly proclaim that nothing lives in this world but Truth.

We can not realize Rama by reading the Ramayana or Krishna by reading the Gita or Allah by reading the Koran or Christ by reading the Bible; the only means of realizing them is by developing a pure and noble character. Character is based on virtuous action and virtuous action is grounded on Truth. Truth, then, is the source and foundation of all things that are good and great.

—Mahatma Gandhi

The seeker of Truth will be humble to the core. Gandhi's own words will reveal this better.

The seeker after Truth should be humbler than the dust. The world crushes the dust under its feet, but the seeker after Truth should so humble himself that even the dust could crush him. Only then, and not till then, will he have a glimpse of Truth.

—Mahatma Gandhi

A seeker of Truth can not be a hypocrite. His life will be an open book. The ugly face of hypocrisy that we frequently come across in many places is due to the fact that people lack faith on Truth. One who seeks Truth will have harmony of thought, word and deed.

Always aim at complete harmony of thought, word and deed.

—Mahatma Gandhi

The above quote of Gandhi has its base in Truth. When one follows Truth, one can not think and act differently. It will be simply impossible for one who follows Truth to say one thing and to do some other thing that is opposite to what he said. Harmony of thought, word and deed is a must for a leader to be successful. We come across many great personalities who declare that words and deeds should not differ. One should 'walk the talk' is the maxim that we normally come across. But Gandhi goes one step further. He demands harmony not only between word and deed but also between thought and word. Because, if one thinks what one does not utter (or utters what one does not think), it is against Truth. And Gandhi can not accept this. Hence, he demands harmony of thought, word and deed. And this is a great lesson that a business executive can learn from Gandhi.

When a leader maintains harmony of thought, word and deed he will be respected by all – by his peers, by his subordinates, by his customers and even by his competitors. This gives him a great credibility and his stature will improve. By remaining true to his thoughts, words and deeds, a leader can instill confidence among his team members to come out openly and express their views on any issue without any sense of hesitation and this will improve communication between the team members a lot and will not give room for gossips and doubts.

Honest differences are often a healthy sign of progress.

—Mahatma Gandhi

Differences of opinions will come out only if every team member strongly believes that every other member is true to his thoughts, words and deeds. And an organization in which the members of a team have such a level of confidence with their team leader and with their colleagues is bound to succeed because differences of opinions will be welcome in such a team and the differences will be understood and ironed out as everyone will believe that every other person is true to his thought and word and that there is nothing wrong about that.

Compassion

As we have seen, compassion is the binding force that unites a group. Compassion should be towards the humanity at large; in fact it should be directed towards all living beings on the earth. A leader can not be compassionate only towards his team members. It is simply not possible. One who is compassionate will be compassionate towards all, towards all living beings. He will be compassion personified. Such a vision will be possible when one looks at all living beings as his fellow beings.

Gandhi is against sin, but is not against sinners. This is because a sinner is a human being and a compassionate person can not be against any human being, be he a saint or a sinner. Compassion is universal and it can not distinguish between persons.

Hate the sin, love the sinner.

—Mahatma Gandhi

Gandhi is very firm that human beings, per se are good. There can be some one here and there who is not up to the mark, who is least bothered about committing sin, who is selfish to the core, who does not love his fellow beings. But, this can not be without reason. Such a person might have been born and brought up under conditions that have made him behave so. He can be transformed into a perfect human being. It is very much possible. All that is required is giving proper vision to the person. Mahatma Gandhi could embrace people of different views and opinions because he had faith in humanity.

You must not lose faith in humanity. Humanity is an ocean. If a few drops of the ocean are dirty, the ocean does not become dirty.

—Mahatma Gandhi

Mahatma Gandhi's compassion towards humanity has its base rooted in *Ahimsa* (non-violence) and Gandhi is a strong advocate of *Ahimsa.* By *Ahimsa*, Gandhi meant the eradication of the desire to injure or kill. Gandhi regarded *Ahimsa* as the means and Truth as his ultimate goal. The non-violence practiced by Gandhi was not only abstaining from physical violence against any living being but also abstaining from any type of mental, verbal and functional negativity against anyone. The views of

Mahatma Gandhi are in tune with that of Gautama Buddha and are very much relevant in today's world to bring about peaceful co-existence.

Compassion is the cream of religion. Absolute wisdom is absolute compassion. Without this healing touch of our loving compassion for one and all, even if we make the whole world flowing with milk and honey, widespread misery and suffering in one form or the other will prevail on earth as ever before.

—Gautama Buddha

Humility

Humility has been emphasized as a noble quality of a human being for a very long time. In fact, the emphasis on humility is as old as religion and all religions regard humility as a great virtue of a religious person. Humility and leadership go hand in hand. Great leaders the world has seen were and have been very humble personalities. From out of their humility they inspire, motivate and inspire those they lead. A leader gains the confidence of his followers when he shows to them that he is ever ready to accept his errors and mistakes. It becomes his strength to confess. It exposes the sincerity and frankness of the leader and his stature increases in the minds of his followers and this becomes a great strength for the leader. But the point not to be missed is that a great leader does not remain humble to gain the confidence of his followers or any thing like that. He is humble because he loves everyone around; he is humble because he is compassionate towards all. It is an expression of love.

Let us see some of the uttering of Gandhi that stand testimony to his humility.

I claim to be a simple individual liable to err like any other fellow mortal. However, I have humility enough to confess my errors and retrace my steps.

—Mahatma Gandhi

Confession of errors is like a broom which sweeps away the dirt and leaves the surface brighter and cleaner. I feel stronger for confession.

—Mahatma Gandhi

It is unwise to be too sure of one's own wisdom. It is healthy to be reminded that the strongest might weaken and the wisest might err.

—Mahatma Gandhi

Nishkama Karma

Gandhi has set a good example for performing *nishkama karma.* He performed his actions, without anticipation of anything in return. He performed actions for actions' sake and put forth his fullest efforts. But he left the results to God. Being an ardent follower of the Bhagavad Gita, it was not difficult for him to perform his actions putting forth every thing he has, yet leaving the results to be decided by God. His approach towards work is revealed by his following uttering.

Infinite striving to be the best is man's duty; it is its own reward. Everything else is in God's hands.

—Mahatma Gandhi

I do not want to foresee the future. I am concerned with taking care of the present. God had given me no control over the moment following.

—Mahatma Gandhi

Gandhi could perform his duties with a sense of detachment, without any anticipation about the results. This is because of his strong, unshakeable faith in God.

There is nothing that wastes the body like worry and one who has any faith in God should be ashamed to worry about anything whatsoever.

—Mahatma Gandhi

The above words of Gandhi reveal the secret behind his success. Any one can learn a great lesson on leading a stress-free life from the above words of Gandhi. When he says that one should be ashamed of worrying about anything if one has faith in God, he touches the peak of surrendering everything to the divine will which is called *saranagathi* in Hinduism and is considered as the ultimate path to God-realisation. In the Bhagavad Gita, Lord Krishna declares *saranagathi* as *paramam guhyam* (supreme secret).

Taking People Along

Gandhi led a great nation. It was team with people from different parts of the country, people with different ideologies, people belonging to different faiths. Yet, he could lead them from the front with success, because he knew that leading means getting along with people.

I suppose leadership at one time meant muscles, but today it means getting along with people.

—Mahatma Gandhi

Man becomes great exactly in the degree in which he works for the welfare of his fellow-men.

—Mahatma Gandhi

Now, we know the secret behind his success. Yes, he took people along with him, gaining their confidence. But it is easier said than done. It requires great qualities and enormous will-power. But, Mahatma Gandhi could accomplish this task since he made his life a selfless service to humanity.

O Bharata, the ignorant ones, desirous of personal good, perform actions with sensory attachment. But, the wise work with an impersonal attitude and spiritual vision for the good of all beings.

—The Bhagavad Gita

The Gita says that the wise would be good to all beings, not just to mankind alone. This is because, any one who offers selfless service will have a spiritual vision in which he could not distinguish between one form of life and another. For him, all living beings are equal. Gandhi's vision is not far from this as we could see from what he says.

The good man is the friend of all living beings.

—Mahatma Gandhi

4. Conclusion

India has been fortunate enough for having given birth to the great soul Mahatma Gandhi. Gandhi has left to the world a great message of following Truth and Non-violence. He is a rare personality who lived his words. Though he preached no religion, he is more religious than most other religious personalities in the sense that he had been a relentless pursuer of Truth and let his life to be his message for the future generations to come. At the end, let us contemplate on what Gandhi had to say in searching for God.

If you don't find God in the next person you meet, it is a waste of time looking for Him further.

—Mahatma Gandhi

Gunas form component parts of everything evolved, but in varying proportions, one or other being in excess. In other words, they affect everything in creation unequally; and as they affect man, make him divine and noble, thoroughly human and selfish or bestial and ignorant according to the predominance of goodness, passion or darkness respectively. The soul, on the other hand, though bound by the Gunas, is itself wholly and entirely free from such constituent ingradients and it is nir-guna.

—The Sankhya Philosophy

9 CHAPTER

Transactional Analysis–An Indian Perspective

In the state of Sattva, a man is neither satisfied by fulfilling his physical desires nor contented to remain within the limits of his intellect, but stands steadily keeping the balance between both. In this state alone he can discriminate properly. Sattva gives equilibrium and enables us to think and act rightly.

—Swami Paramananda

1. INTRODUCTION

Communication between people at work assumes greater importance in any organization. As the size of an organization increases, it becomes increasingly difficult to ensure that communication is free from distortion. When human beings interact with one another, a social transaction takes place. Eric Berne (1910 – 1970), a renowned psychiatrist developed Transactional Analysis, which is a study of social transaction between people. The objective of Transactional Analysis is to provide a better understanding of how people relate to each other so that they may develop improved communication among themselves. After the development of the theory of Transactional Analysis in 1950s, it has gained wider recognition and is now being used in psychotherapy and in organizations where a better understanding of communication and improvement in communication between the organizational members are desired. A team leader who wants to make an impact can not ignore the message contained in Transactional Analysis as it deals with communication between individuals and for smooth functioning of an organization proper communication is a *sine qua nun*. Before going to see what the Indian wisdom has to say on the process of communication between individuals, it will be in order if we have a quick glimpse of Transactional Analysis proposed by Eric Berne.

2. TRANSACTIONAL ANALYSIS (TA)

Berne identified that the human personality is made up of three ego states and that human behaviour is based on these ego states. Thus, the ego states help explain how individuals are made up and how they interact with one another. The three ego states identified by Berne are the parent ego state, the adult ego state and the child ego state. According to Berne, the parent ego state is the result of conditioning of mind that is brought about on the basis of the messages received by people during their early childhood from their parents and parent figures (like elder brothers, sisters, teachers etc.). These messages given by parents and parent figures get registered in the minds of the child and these recorded impressions mould the child's personality. When a person is in a parent ego state, he/she interacts with others deriving inspiration from the pool of recorded impressions made in him/her by parents and parent figures. A person interacting from parent ego state is dogmatic, protective, evaluative, autocratic and righteous. The Adult ego state is the result of rational thinking. It is the result of data gathering, data processing and data analysis. The adult takes the emotional content of the child and the value laden content of the parent, to check them out in the reality of the external world, before arriving at the desired behaviour pattern. Thus, the Adult ego state is logical, rational and unemotional and a person interacting from the Adult ego state will exhibit these qualities. The Child ego state includes feelings of frustration, inadequacy and helplessness that are inevitable part of one's childhood. Berne believed that such recordings in the Child ego state occur from childbirth up to the age of about five years. The Child ego state is selfish and rebellious. At times, it is also creative. Thus, when a person interacts from his/her Child ego state, he/she exhibits these characteristics that reflect his/her early childhood conditions.

Berne believed that each one of us use all the three ego states during our interaction; we are switching between the three ego state all the time, but prefer to be in one of the ego states especially. Though all of us transact from all the three ego states from time to time, each one of us generally tends to have a dominant ego state from which we transact most of the time. According to TA, when two persons transact with each other, each remaining in the same ego state, the transaction between the two will be 'parallel'. 'Parallel' transactions are also called complementary transactions. In complementary transactions, the parties to the transaction are at the same mental wave length. TA concludes that Adult – to – Adult transaction (i.e., when a person transacts with another in Adult ego state and the respondent also reacts in Adult ego state) is the most effective for organizations as this type of transaction treats people as equals, improves their understanding and helps to arrive at rational decisions. Though the Adult – to – Adult transaction is the most desired one, other 'parallel' transactions are also acceptable if both the persons in the transaction develop a workable relationship. On the other hand, if the ego states of the two persons engaged in a transaction are different, the transaction will be 'crossed' or 'non-complementary'. Non-complementary transactions are not desired as they block and distort communications. The schematic representation given below depicts parallel and crossed transactions between two individuals.

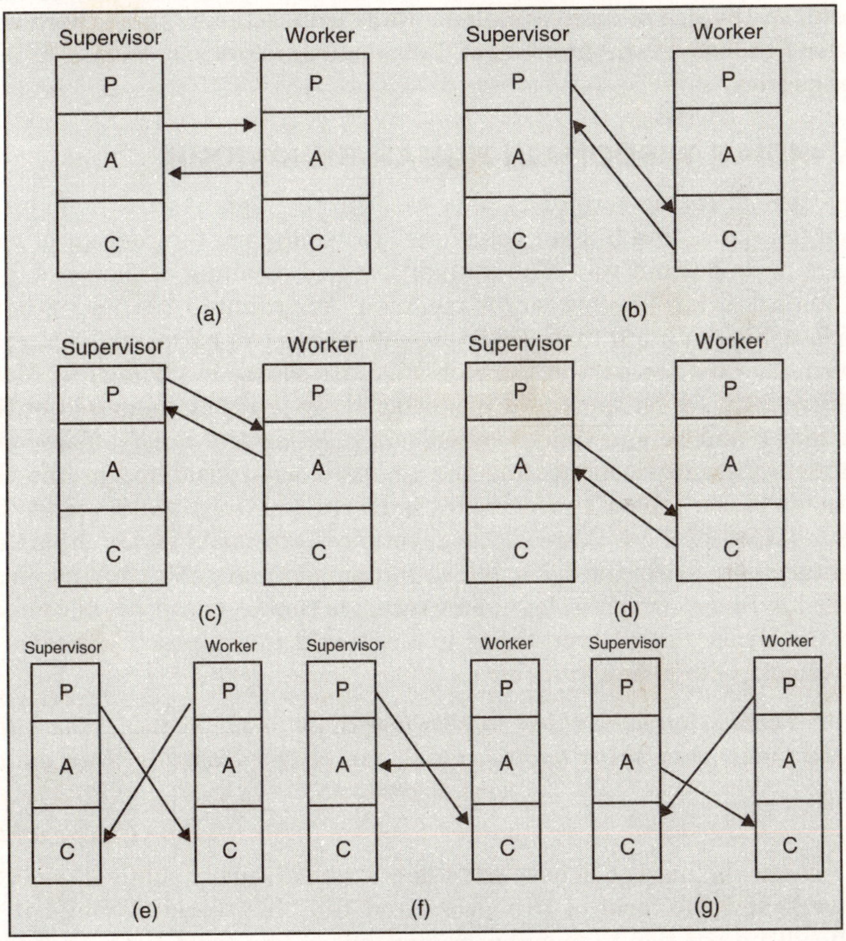

Organizational Behavior

Legend:

P	→ Parent
A	→ Adult
C	→ Child
(a)	→ Most desired transaction
(b), (c), (d)	→ Acceptable transactions
(a), (b), (c), (d)	→ Parrallel or complementary transactions
(e), (f), (g)	→ Undersired transactions
(e), (f), (g)	→ Crossed or non-complementary transactions

Though TA has helped to analyze the transaction pattern between two individuals, it has not been proved beyond doubt that training the employees in TA will improve the level of parallel transactions in an organization. W.W. Burke, professor of psychology, Teachers College, Columbia University who did extensive studies on this aspect concluded that there is no hard, empirically established evidence that training in TA does result in the use of more complementary transactions. Thus, there arises a need to look at the problem of Transactional Analysis from a different perspective.

3. INDIAN WISDOM ON HUMAN BEHAVIOUR

The age-old Indian scriptures have in them the highest wisdom on human characteristics and human behaviour. In Hinduism, the concept of *gunas* plays an important role. The straightforward meaning of the word *'guna'* is quality. It has another subtle meaning. According to *Sankhya* School of philosophy, the world that we see around us has two parts, viz., matter and spirit. The matter part of the world has its source in *prakriti* or Mother nature from which the world has evolved. *Prakiriti* is composed of three extremely subtle substances called *sattva*, *rajas* and *tamas*. These three subtle substances constituting the *prakiriti* are considered as the three strands of the rope of *prakiriti*. In Sanskrit, the word *'guna'* stands for a strand. Hence, these three subtle substances are called *gunas*. Apart from matter, there exists the spirit, which contains innumerable sentient entities called *purusha*, which in lay-man's terms is soul. As *prakiriti* is composed on the three *gunas*, everything in the world is composed of them. The Bhagavad Gita affirms this idea.

There is no such thing in this world, or in the heaven, where live the Devas with shiny bodies, which can be free from the three gunas born of prakiriti.

—The Bhagavad Gita

It may be hard to believe as to how such extremely subtle *gunas* could have taken the form of this gross and tangible world. Though it is a difficult proposition to imagine, science has of late come out with findings in support of this concept. Albert Einstein's theory of relativity shows that energy and mass are the same thing and that neither one appears without the other. The existence of gunas can not be directly perceived because of their extreme subtlety. But, they are present in any and every thing in the world. It is these *gunas* that bind *purusha* to the body

....Sattva, rajas, tamas – these gunas, O mighty-armed, born of prakiriti, bind the immutable embodied being to the body.

—The Bhagavad Gita

The qualities of the *gunas* differ. *Sattva-guna* is of the nature of pleasure, joy, purity, happiness and tranquility. *Rajas* causes activity, movement, restlessness, anger, pride, vanity, desire to dominate etc., *Tamas* is born of ignorance, inertia and sluggishness. Though all the three *gunas* are present in each individual, only one of the three *gunas* dominates and the individual behaves according to the *guna* that is dominant.

....Sattva asserts itself, O Bharata, by predominating over Rajas and Tamas; and Tamas over Sattva and Tamas; and Tamas over Sattva and Rajas.

—The Bhagavad Gita

Since the individuals differ in their guna, their perception differs. A same incident or happening is perceived and interpreted differently by different persons. Hence, each individual reacts differently to the same situation.

......The same physical sight, landscape or creation in general, animate or inanimate, may be perceived differently by persons with different dominant gunas.

—The Bhagavad Gita

The behaviour pattern of persons with different dominant *gunas* is explained in the Bhagavad Gita in clear terms.

....Greed, activity, the undertaking of actions and delusion – these arise, O best of Bharatas, where Rajas is predominant.........

.....Indiscrimination, inertness, heedlessness and delusion – these arise, O joy of Kurus, when Tamas is predominant......

.....When the light of knowledge beams through all the gateways of the body, then it may be known that Sattva is predominant.

—The Bhagavad Gita

Studying the personality of an individual on the basis of the *guna* that dominates him/her will throw light on his/her behaviour pattern. A person who has dominance of *Sattva guna* will be loving, compassionate and interested in the welfare of others. He will be able to discriminate correctly between right and wrong, between those that are permanent and that are fleeting. Since such a person will love all, he can not hate anyone. He will have the qualities of fearlessness, uprightness, purity, truthfulness, forgiveness and absence of anger and passions. He can not hate another person who has *Rajas* or *Tamas* domination, because he can not distinguish between individuals. In fact, he can not distinguish between human and other living beings and for him all beings are equal. He will be compassion personified. Such a person will be a great asset to an organization. Because of his compassionate and accommodative nature, his transactions with all others in the organization will be parallel. He can not have crossed transaction with anyone. A *Sattvik* person will not get offended while transacting/communicating with a *Rajasik* or *Tamasik* personality. The transaction between a *Sattvik* and a *Rajasik* person will be complementary. So also will be the transaction between a *Sattvik* and a *Tamasik* person. On the other hand, transactions between two *Rajasik* persons will be crossed. Similarly, transactions between two *Tamasik* person will also be crossed. Transactions between a *Rajasik* and a *Tamasik* person will in all probability be crossed. This is because, both *Rajasik* and *Tamasik* personalities will not appreciate the views of others and the result will be a blockage of communication. Transactions between a *Rajasik* and a *Tamasik* person suffer because the *Rajasik* person will be highly dominating and ego-centric while the *Tamasik* person will exhibit high level of ignorance and foolishness. Based on the above understanding, we can immediately arrive at the simple inference that if an organization has

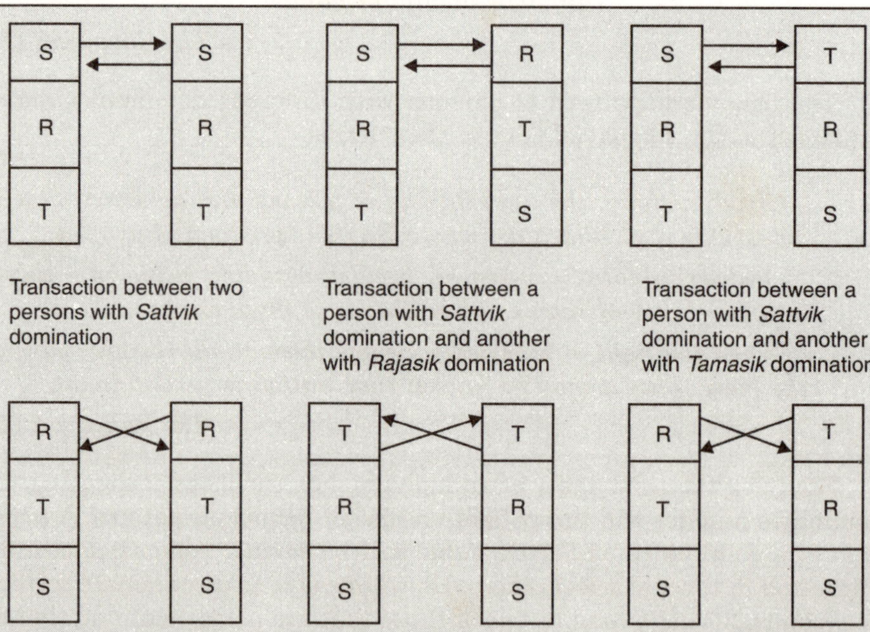

Transaction between two persons with *Sattvik* domination

Transaction between a person with *Sattvik* domination and another with *Rajasik* domination

Transaction between a person with *Sattvik* domination and another with *Tamasik* domination

Transaction between two persons with *Rajasik* domination

Transaction between two persons with *Tamasik* domination

Transaction between a person with *Rajasik* domination and another with *Tamasik* domination

Legend: R-*Rajasik* domination; T-*Tamasik* domination; S-*Sattvik* domination

a larger proportion of *Rajasik* and *Tamasik* personalities, it will be a difficult task to ensure harmony and synergy in the group and communication between the group members will suffer a lot.

The schematic representation given below depicts parallel and crossed transactions between two individuals who are dominated by the same and by different *gunas*.

4. NEED TO CULTIVATE *SATTVIK GUNA* AMONG TEAM MEMBERS

Among the barriers to communication, mental barrier is the toughest one. It is the most difficult one to overcome. Other barriers can be removed, but not the mental barriers. We come across this quite frequently in social interactions. One can be a good receiver of a message, only if one is not prejudiced. And this can happen only if there is no mental barrier. However, since people differ in their *gunas*, their perception differs. This difference in perception leads to different views and opinions, leading to prejudiced positions. A *Sattvik* person, by nature is more accommodative and more considerate. Hence, he will not form prejudiced views. Though he may have his own ideals, he will be a compassionate listener of others' views. The more the number of persons with *Sattvik guna* in a team, the better will be the transaction/communication between the team members.

The Bhagavad Gita advocates humanity to rise from the lower level of *Tamas* and *Rajas gunas* to the higher level of the *Sattva guna*. Lord Krishna utters the following to *Arjuna* in the *Gita*.

> ...... *Sattva, Rajas and Tamas are the three modes of material nature dealt by Vedas. Be ever Sattvik, constant in peace and harmony, without ambition to acquire or secure, be soulful, self-conscious...*
>
> —*The Bhagavad Gita*

Hence, a leader should be more involved in transforming the team members who show tendencies of *Rajasik* and *Tamasik* domination into *Sattvik* personalities. The leader has to give more importance to achieve this transformation among his team members. While training the team members in acquiring work related skills, the leader should not loose sight of the vital aspect of imparting moral values in them, thus making them become more and more *Sattvik* in their approach to the world around. Then, improvement of the level of complementary transactions among the members will follow as a natural consequence and the team will act as a coherent one with improved synergy. A *Sattvik* person will be glad when others are happy. He won't and in fact he can't feel jealous in the joy of others.

5. CONCLUSION

Eric Berne's study does not take cognizance of the inborn qualities with which a person comes to the world. According to Berne, people acquire three different ego states based on their acquired stimulus from the surroundings. He has not considered inborn qualities of human beings. The Indian way of classifying personalities on the basis of their dominant *guna* goes deep into the process of evolution of life. Inborn qualities are also, in a way acquired qualities, the mode of acquisition being through the genes. Thus, the classification of persons into categories of *Rajasik, Tamasik* and *Sattvik* attitudes is more realistic and broad-based. The strength of Indian wisdom lies in its inference that the three types of *gunas* are due to the influence of *prakiriti* and that the *Atman* that is engrossed by these three *gunas* is unaffected and free from the influence of *gunas*. Though Indian scriptures regard *Sattvik guna* as the one that is desired to be acquired by a human being, it does not stop there. The purpose of the elaborate description of the three *gunas* in *The Bhagavad Gita* and in other scriptures is not merely to encourage one to become a *Sattvik* personality. Becoming a *Sattvik* personality is a means to an end and not an end in itself. The aim of the Gita is to make man understand the nature of the three *gunas* and how they keep us in bondage and illusion. By cultivating *Sattva guna* one overcomes passion (which is the attribute of the *Rajas*) and ignorance (which is the attribute of the *Tamas*) which will help one to reach higher levels of coinsciousness.

When the embodied being is able to transcend these three modes (gunas), he can become free from birth, death, old age and their distress and can enjoy nectar even in this life.

—*The Bhagavad Gita*

To Arjuna's question as to what the marks of those who have transcended the three modes of material Nature, Lord Krishna answers in *The Bhagavad Gita* as under:

One transcends the modes of material nature who neither hates the presence of enlightenment, activity, and delusion; nor desires for them when they are absent; who remains like a witness without being affected by the modes (gunas) of material Nature (prakiriti); who stays firmly attached to the Lord without wavering – thinking that only the modes of material Nature (gunas of prakiriti) are operating. And one depends on the Lord and is indifferent to pain and pleasure; to who a clod, a stone and gold are alike; to whom the dear and the unfriendly are alike; who is of firm mind; who is calm in censure and in praise and indifferent to honour and disgrace; who is impartial to friend and foe; and who has renounced the sense of doership.

—The Bhagavad Gita

Thus, while Indian wisdom on human behaviour has its roots on the subtle aspects of nature's influence on man, it requires one to understand as to how one is tied to this worldly bondage, expects one to realize that the *Atman* that is engrossed by the three *gunas* of nature is totally free from the three *gunas* and explains the state of total indifference that can be reached by realizing the illusionary play of Nature, thus leading one to self realization.

It is most difficult to define Dharma. Dharma has been explained to be that which helps the uplifment of living beings. Therefore, that which ensures the welfare of living beings is surely Dharma. The learned Rishis have declared that which sustains is Dharma.

—Shanthi Parva/The Mahabharata

10
CHAPTER

Dharma and its Relevance to Leaders

The root of Dharma is compassion
—Tulsidass

1. INTRODUCTION

The word '*Dharma*' is derived from the Sanskrit root '*Dhri*' which means 'to hold'. Hence, as per etymological meaning, *Dharma* refers to that which holds this entire world. In other words, *Dharma* is what that holds the people of the world. According to Hinduism, *Dharma* is the all-powerful law of God that holds together and sustains the entire universe. *Dharma* is the foundation of the Indian way of life – both religious and secular. Ancient Indian seers and sages have seen *Dharma* as the law that governs the universe and that affects everything in collective and individual levels in order to lead every being to perfection. It is the law through which everything in the universe, starting from micro-organism to macro galaxies evolve to higher planes. The concept of *Dharma* is unique to Indian religious system and it is a unified law that is applicable to all beings on the earth. In the process of evolution, according to Indian spiritual system, man reaches perfection on attaining self-realisation. Since the universal law of Dharma aids in evolution of all beings on the earth, it can be inferred that anything that helps human beings attain self-realisation is *Dharma*. The opposite of *Dharma* is *Adharma* which is anything that hinders attaining self-realisation. Since self-realisation is considered as the ultimate goal of all spiritual pursuits, living as per *Dharmic* path is considered as the righteous living. The universal law of *Dharma*, though has self-realisation as its ultimate goal, does not ignore the life and the way of living at the present. In fact, it is through living life in the righteous way, one is expected to reach greater heights in spiritual advancement, at which one might realize the self. Hence, adherence to Dharma, not only leads one self-realisation (or at least takes one to a stage that is conducive for realizing the self), but also paves way for experiencing peace, joy, strength and tranquility within one's self, till one lives his/her life on the earth. Thus, *Dharma* is the fundamental law that every human being is expected to follow while living on this earth that will help in reaching higher stages in the process of evolution.

2. THE PATH OF *DHARMA*

The virtues required for leading a *Dharmic* way of life are available in the form of codes/rules of conduct at many places in the vast spiritual literature of India.

According to *Bhagavat Purana,* for righteous living, i.e., for leading life on the path of *Dharma,* one has to possess the following four qualities:

Austerity (tap)
Purity (shauch)
Compassion (daya)
&
Truthfulness (satya)

Manusmriti prescribes the following ten rules for the observance of Dharma.

Patience (dhriti)
Forgiveness (kshama)
Piety or self-control (dama)
Honesty (asteya)
Sanctity (shauch)
Control of senses (indraiya-nigrah)
Reason (dhi)
Learning (vidya)
Truthfulness (satya)
Absence of anger (krodha)

Padma purana quotes that *Dharma* proceeds from continence, truthfulness, austerity, charity, self-control, forbearance, purity, non-violence, serenity and non-thieving. According to *Matsya purana,* freedom from malice, absence of covetousness, control of the senses, austerity, celibacy, truthfulness, forbearance and fortitude constitute the fundamentals of *Sanatana Dharma*. ('*sanatana*' refers to 'eternal').*Vishnu purana* quotes forgiveness, truthfulness, control of the mind, purity, practice of charity, control of the senses, non-violence, service to the Guru, visiting holy places, compassion, simplicity, absence of greed etc., as the aspects of Samanya Dharma. ('*samanya*' refers to 'general law applicable to all men').

From the above, we could find that compassion, truthfulness, purity and self-control run as a common thread among the virtues prescribed by different spiritual literatures.

Compassion is like fragrance from a flower. It will spread all around the flower and whosoever comes near the flower can feel it. A person who is compassionate towards all living beings is like a sweet smelling flower spreading its fragrance to all those who come near. It is a great quality required of a leader. Subordinates and colleagues will feel comfortable in the presence of a leader who is compassionate. If one is compassionate, he/she will be ever prepared to help others.

If it is one man's karma to suffer, isn't it our Dharma to help ease his suffering and pain?

—Maa Amritanandamayi

Truthfulness is another great virtue required of a leader. Truth must be observed in thought, word and deed. If a leader observes truth in his thought, word and deed, he will command respect and credibility, which will make him build an effective team with ease.

Purity refers to purity of mind. A person with pure mind will be innocent, frank, unbiased and straightforward and will be free from evil thoughts. Purity of mind will make one tranquil and will free one from carrying unwanted burden of worries and anxieties. A leader with pure mind is a great asset for any organization because he will be taking right decisions, unaffected by external influences.

Self-control implies patience, forbearance, endurance and annihilation of ego coupled with humility. One who has self-control will be prepared to sacrifice his/her comforts for the welfare of the organization and the organizational members. When a leader possesses this quality, there is nothing like that.

It may so happen that at times we might come across a situation where it would be difficult to decide upon as to which the path of *Dharma* is. A leader will be required to decide a course of action, weighing the options available and considering the pros and cons of the options. The options may be so complicated that it would be difficult to decide upon the right choice. The leader who wants to follow the *Dharmic* path may find it difficult to decide on the choice. Under such situations, the rule to be followed is that Dharma is that path which gives joy and peace to all. The following words of Satya Sai Baba will act as the guiding force under such situations.

How are you to decide in any particular case what Dharma and what is not? That which does not inflict pain on you and others – that is Dharma. This follows from the recognition that same God resides in everyone and if you injure another, you are hurting the same God who is in you. Dharma enables you to come to the recognition that anything that is bad for another is also bad for you. So, act in such a way that you get joy and others too get joy. Or take another standard for your actions. Make the mind, the speech and body agree in harmony. Act as you speck, speak as you feel, do not play false to your conscience. That is the Dharmic way of life.

—Satya Sai Baba

3. CONCLUSION

Life is a series of experiences. This body is the vehicle in which man performs his journey of life. In his journey, man gains various and varied experiences. And finally, when a person departs from this earth, he experiences death. Death is not and can not be the end of all. Even death is an experience in life. After death, the Experiencer travels on to the next stage in the unbroken chain of experiences. Finally, the Experiencer realizes that he is different from the experiences that he had undergone, that he is really the Spirit or *Atman* that has all along been conditioned by matter. On realizing this, he becomes one with the existence – he merges with the existence. There are no two things at this stage. All the illusions of one undergoing different experiences are due to conditioning of matter. When the Spirit breaks open the illusionary envelope created by conditioning of matter, the Spirit realizes the Truth and merges with the Almighty. Majority of religions, more or less agree with this view of Hinduism though they may define in different terms. Words are inadequate to define the Absolute. The Absolute or the Almighty can only be experienced and can not be expressed. Expressing the Absolute will only be a futile attempt, since words are incapable of expressing. Yet, the search for knowing the Truth, the search for knowing what lies beyond after one's life on the earth ends, the search for knowing 'Who am I?' goes on for ever and man's quest towards this will never come to an end.

The search for realizing the Truth, the urge for knowing the unknown is present inherently in every living being. But, when man gets caught in the web of materialism and the Spirit gets enclosed by the shield of conditioning of matter, man suppresses his urge to know the Truth and gets involved in gaining material pleasures, though knowing well that such pleasures are impermanent in nature, with the result that man has progressed in the external world and has not progressed internally. Internally, every one will find an unfilled vacuum in spite of the so called progress and prosperity attained externally. The situation can not remain status-quo for long. Man has started realizing gradually that material progress will not lead him to attain contentment and happiness. Man has started looking inwards. It is here that *Dharma* has its role to play. When one is sincere and steadfast to know the Truth, to realize the self, he is guided by the spiritual literatures to follow the path of *Dharma.* Following the path of Dharma will ensure one lead a happy, joyful, peaceful and contented life here on the earth and to merge with the Ultimate after quitting the physical body.

One who follows the path of *Dharma* will set an example for others to emulate. People will find in a person who follows *Dharmic* way of life, something unique and will get attracted to him/her. A person who follows *Dharma* will radiate an aura of happiness around that will register strong impressions in the minds of those who come into contact with the person. The impressions formed will be so strong that the person will be remembered for long. A leader who follows the path of Dharma will be remembered by his team-mates, subordinates and peers for a long time since in such a leader, they would have identified a role model to emulate. If a leader is remembered and the memories are cherished by his subordinates, peers and team members for the *Dharmic* qualities that the leader possessed, it can be said the leader has spent his life purposefully.

Rama, Krishna, Buddha, Mahavir and Jesus still live in the form of the ideals that they cherished in their life time and the righteous path that they treaded along throughout their journey of life. When Rama was about to depart to the forest to spend fourteen years in exile, Kausalya, Rama's mother blessed Rama, saying, "Oh Rama, let that righteousness (*Dharma*) which you are fostering with courage and discipline, protect you." Yes. Indian religious scriptures strongly affirm that *Dharma* protects one while living on this earth and accompanies after departing from here. Leaders who tread the path of *Dharma* will lead a peaceful and purposeful life, will leave an indelible, soothing impression in the minds of their team members, colleagues and subordinates and will remain in their heart for ever and there is no other way by which this can be achieved.

Action coupled with meditation, japa, chanting and other spiritual practices are the means to attain the state of selflessness. There should always be a balance between meditation and action. Action alone can not take you to the goal. Action performed with an attitude of self-surrender and love is the right path.

—Maa Amritanandamayi

CHAPTER 11

TQM, A People's Movement

Service is a life time program; it knows no rest or respite. This body has been given to you so that you may devote its strength and skills to the service of brother-man. Serve man until you see God in all men; then what you do will be elevated to worship.

—Satya Sai Baba

1. INTRODUCTION

All organizations survive on customer satisfaction. Customer satisfaction with regard to a product or service is all pervasive; it covers design, reliability, performance, robustness, efficiency, aesthetics and price of a product/service. It also includes continuous improvement of quality that benefits the customers. Dr. W. Edwards Deming who is one of the pioneers of quality movement suggested a continuous quality improvement solution model that follows the following cycle:

Improvement in quality → Increase in productivity → Reduction in cost → Reduction in price → Increased market share → Sustenance in business → Creation of more jobs and increased return on investment. The cycle is repeated by further improvement in quality.

J.M. Juran, another quality expert, who also recommends continuous improvement in quality, talks about 'managerial breakthrough'. Juran believed that the prime cause for the failure of organizations is faulty systems controlled by the management. Management breakthrough is a situation in which the management realizes that the present level of performance is not good enough and that there requires to be something done about it. On this realization, the management should aim at achieving improved performance, through quality improvement and other means. The management should identify and eliminate any obstacle that exists as a hindrance to quality improvement.

Philip B. Crosby who did pioneering work on cost of quality said that quality is free. He emphasized that it is always cheaper to do the job right first time. One of the important principles supported by Crosby is that 'in discussing quality, we are dealing with a people situation'. Crosby emphasized that bringing about changes in attitudes of people at all levels in the organization is vital for the successful implementation any quality improvement programme and that management has the responsibility in bringing about this change of attitude throughout the organization and this is possible only when the attitudinal change starts first at the management level.

Total Quality Management (TQM), is thus an approach for management and employees to be involved in. It requires a cultural change in the organization at all levels and without an attitudinal change in the minds of all the organizational members, achieving total quality might as well remain only as a pleasant dream. Because, it is through people any programme gets implemented.

2. BEHAVIORAL BARRIER

The two barriers identified that pose a threat for the successful implementation of TQM in any organization are:

- Organizational barrier
- Behavioral barrier

Organizational barriers are visible. They are in the form of lack of commitment by the top management, improper planning, lack of training and education, incompatible organizational structure etc., Since these barriers are visible they can be identified and corrected. But, behavioral barriers are difficult to identify and difficult to overcome. Total quality can be possible only when both the barriers are overcome. Peter Wicken's comments in *"The Road to Nissan"* is worth noting here.

"In summary, the quality of work will only be high if the individual is fully motivated. While we may say that quality must be 'built into' the job, this will only happen if the right attitude for quality comes from within the individual. No amount of exhortation will achieve genuine commitment to quality – wall posters and slogans will fail. It is a key management responsibility and can be obtained only if we realize that it is total motivation that matters."

The behavioral barrier occurs because of people's reluctance to change. They might even agree with the urgent need to bring about quality in all aspects of the organization's functioning. But, still people may not participate wholeheartedly in the quality movement. This is seen in many instances. The reason that can be attributed is that people have a tendency to resist change, irrespective of whether the change is for good or bad. When people resist change, what could be the reason for that? Any change management programme, if conducted without understanding the attitude of the people involved is not expected to yield the desired results. Even if a programme has been successful in effecting the required changes among the people, it may be only short-lived and may prevail for a few months, few weeks or a few days and people may again go back to their comfort zones. This happens in every organization and management trainers are hard to find a permanent solution. It remains a very tough task before them – to make people accept changes that are considered good for the organization. But then, why do people resist changes? A right solution can be conceived of only if the root cause of the problem is known. If we observe any situation in life where people show resistance to change, we could see that they find themselves uncomfortable in the changed situation. People prefer to stay in comfort zones because they are familiar with the situation; they won't be taken for a surprise; they won't face any unexpected shock. So, even if things in the comfort zones are not conducive for their physical, mental and emotional wellbeing, still people prefer to stick to known pattern of life. If they are to choose the unknown, unfamiliar path, there can always be some sort of anxiety. When accepting a change, they throw themselves open to the influence of unknown forces and situations. And this brings a sense of insecurity and people find themselves uncomfortable.

One can accept the changes brought about in an organization if one is prepared to bear with the inconveniences that the intended changes might cause. One can accept the inconveniences if one derives satisfaction in offering work as a sacrifice. TQM being a concept that requires total involvement of all the organizational members and a total reorientation of their attitudes towards quality, it requires voluntary participation of all the organizational members. Voluntary participation is possible to achieve only if every one of the organizational member understands that his/her very life is the result of sacrifices done by very many people, both known and unknown, by many other living beings on the earth, by the forces of nature that help sustain life on the earth and realizes that he/she has an obligation to make good for what he/she has received. One can offer selfless service only when one realizes his/her indebtedness to the world. Hence, if a management trainer wants to be successful in bringing about the required change, he has to achieve a total mental transformation of the trainees, making them realize that they have an obligation to the world at large. Once man realizes his indebtedness to the whole existence, his attitude towards work will change. Then, any amount of work will not be a burden to him. As he serves more, he will feel more and more relieved of discharging his obligations. Man can not serve the nature. Nature does not expect anything from man though it gives in abundance to man. Man can only serve the humanity. Man can also serve the lower forms of lives to some extent. Hence, selfless service to humanity assumes greater relevance in the context of offering high quality product/service.

The good live for others alone. The wise man should sacrifice himself for others.

—Swami Vivekananda

3. SACRIFICE, THE VIRTUE THAT SUSTAINS

As we have seen, a person's attitude can be changed only if he/she realizes that he/she has already received a lot from the entire existence and has the obligation to pay back to the existence for what has been received. Ancient Indian education system had placed greater emphasis on making the student realize this. Once realized, the student becomes a seasoned human being and will be willing to sacrifice everything he/she has for the welfare of fellow beings. When a society has such individuals who have an attitude to sacrifice, they will offer their physical and mental work for the benefit of the society. For them, work will be worship. When the attitude of work-force in an organization is such, then implementing any change, including implementing TQM in an organization will be a very easy task. Since TQM does nothing but offering to the society a product/service of highest quality, the work-force will take pleasure in contributing their share in the process.

Indian ethos places greater importance to the quality of sacrifice in human life. A verse in the Bhagavad Gita brings out the essence of sacrifice, by giving the example of rain.

All creatures are the product of food, food is the product of rain, rain comes by sacrifice and sacrifice is the noblest form of action.

—Verse-14, Chapter – 3, The Bhagavad Gita

Thirukkural, the book of morals speaks in similar tone.

Duty demands nothing in return;

How can the world recompense rain?

—Verse – 211, Thirukkural

It is rain that sustains life on the earth. Every living being is indebted to rain. The indebtedness is so great that no being can recompense the same. Nature acts in such subtle ways. Clouds do not rain in anticipation of something in return. Man can learn a lot from the clouds. He can learn how to live a meaningful life – how to share without anticipating anything in return – how to distribute whatever one has to all those who need, without any discrimination. Once a person has learnt this simple lesson, his life will become a journey of sacrifice for the welfare of all. Once every employee of an organization is educated to realize his/her indebtedness to the society and to the world at large, then bringing about any change in the work culture of the organization that benefits all the stakeholders including the customers, be it TQM or any other concept, will not pose any problem whatsoever.

The method of doing work as a sacrifice is again brought out in The Bhagavad Gita as under:

In this world people are fettered by action, unless it is performed as a sacrifice. Therefore, O Arjuna, let your acts be done without attachment, as sacrifice only.

—Verse – 9, Chapter – 3, The Bhagavad Gita

4. EXCELLENCE IN DUTY

Excellence refers to perfection. Perfection is an essential feature of nature. If we look around and observe nature as it exists, starting from a tiny grass to a great tree, starting from a single cell organism to the highly evolved human being, we find perfection in their system, in their bodily functions and in every aspect of their metabolism. Only in man-made objects there can be imperfections. In nature, there is no imperfection. Performing one's duty to perfection, with a sense of sacrifice, without expecting anything in return will bring excellence in duty. Lord Krishna says in *The Bhagavad Gita* that excellence in *karma* (i.e., action/ performing one's duty) is *yoga*. According to *Patanjali Maharishi*, *yoga* is stillness of mind. And one can achieve stillness of mind provided one performs actions with a sense of sacrifice for the wellbeing of all, he/she won't be affected by the aftereffects of such actions and will attain stillness of mind. Deming, the quality expert emphasizes that the management of an organization should give first priority to customer satisfaction. And customer satisfaction will become as a by-product if every employee performs his/her part of the job to perfection and produces quality product/ offers quality service, which is possible only if work is performed without any motive, without any attachment but with a sense of sacrifice and with a sense of dedicating it to the Almighty. Every action of a karma yogi will be a selfless service. Selfless service will remove egoism, hatred, jealousy and will promote humility, tolerance and sympathy towards all beings and this in turn calm down the mind from the influences of materialistic thoughts and in the course of time the mind will become gradually still and enter into a meditative stage. At this stage, the person will be performing his/her part of the job to perfection since all his actions will become offerings to the Almighty.

5. PROSPERITY TO ALL

According to *vedic* mythology, every one should work for the good of all. A society can prosper if the individuals in the society prosper. Hence, if every individual works for the prosperity of every other individual, there will be all-round growth and all-round prosperity. Asoka's rock edict speaks about '*sarva loka hitam*' which means 'the well-being of all'. In business parlance, we can say that this is equivalent to 'well-being of all stake holders'. Employees, customers, suppliers, share holders are the stake holders of an organization. Apart from these, the society as a whole is also a stake holder of any organization. If the well-being of all the stake holders is given due consideration by an organization, it will lead to overall growth and prosperity of the society. The view of *vedic* philosophy that every one should work for the welfare of 'all' means that every employee of an organization should work for the welfare of every person in the society. And once an employee's attitude is oriented towards the welfare of the society as a whole, he will willingly put forth his efforts to produce quality products/offer quality service.

6. CONTINUOUS IMPROVEMENT

Deming suggested the PDCA (plan → Do → Check → Act) cycle for continuous improvement of quality. It is a dynamic model and the completion of one turn of the cycle flows into the beginning of the next cycle. It aids in continuous quality improvement. Quality can not be a one-time affair. It needs to be continuously improved which means that every employee in the organization should put forth continuous efforts to improve the quality of the product that the organization produces or the quality of service that the organization offers. A question might arise as to how a person can be prompted to offer his/her best all the time. What is the motivation for one to do so? Obviously, one should be self-motivated to do so. The voluntary efforts that one may put forth in a sense of sacrifice, in a form of presenting the work performed as an offering to the Almighty is to be continued for ever. There can be no stop-gap. This is possible only when a person knows that the secret behind leading a successful life lies in rendering selfless service. Once a person understands this, then he will render selfless service throughout his life time. Such a person, when employed in an organization will keep on working, always keeping in mind that he has to contribute his maximum to the society. If an organization has such employees, Deming's PDCA model will work on its own and it will become a culture of the organization. On the other hand, if the employees are not oriented towards offering selfless service, then implementing PDCA model will require enormous effort on the part of the management and in spite of great efforts the results will only be short lived.

7. CONCLUSION

Implementing TQM or any other quality improvement plan in an organization can succeed if all the employees of the organization, right from the person in the bottom most rung up to the top executive, offer their whole-hearted, voluntary, selfless service towards quality improvement. Such an attitude is possible to attain if one understands that life is spent usefully only when it is spent in the service of others. Almost all religions in the world unanimously agree that service to man is service to God. Hence, if this attitude is inculcated in each and every employee's mind, TQM implementation will be a child's play. Without such an attitude among the employees, it will be an uphill task.

Let us contemplate a verse from the Rig Veda that clearly explains that common vision, universal brotherhood and equitable prosperity for all are required for achieving excellence in life.

O ye mankind,
Let your vision and thinking of life be one and common;
Let your hearts be transpired with feeling of equality;
Let your minds be united together,
resulting in equal prosperity and common excellence in the life for all.

—The Rig Veda

Glossary

Advaida Vedanta	:	A school of Hindu philosophy consolidated by Adi Shankara. According to Advaida Vedanta, Brahman is the only reality and the world, as it appears, is illusory.
Arthasashtra	:	An ancient Indian treatise written by 'Chanakya' on statecraft, economic policy and military strategy.
Arutprakasa Vallalar	:	See 'Vallalar'.
Asana	:	A Sanskrit word for different yoga postures.
Asoka	:	A great Indian emperor (304 B.C. – 232 B.C.) popularly known as 'Ashoka, The great.'
Astavakra	:	A sage who was known to be spiritually well advanced and who is believed to had lived during the period of the epic The Ramayana. He accepted king Janaka as his disciple and gave Janaka instructions about Atman.
Astavakra Gita	:	A treatise on Advaita Vedanta; it is composed in the form of dialogue between the teenager sage Astavakra and his royal disciple, King janaka.
Atman	:	The universal life-principle which is the animator of all organism; it is eternal, unchanging and undistinguishable from the essence of the universe.
Aurobindo	:	Aurobindo Ghosh was born in 1916. He was an Indian nationalist and freedom fighter. He was also a poet, philosopher and yogi.
Auvaiyar	:	A Tamil poetess of the ninth century who lived in the southern parts of India. She was

a revered saint. Her poems were simple but rich in teaching moral values.

Avatar : The descent of a deity to the earth in an incarnate form; the incarnation of a God.

Bhagavad Gita : One of the most important Hindu scriptures. It is a part of 'The Mahabhatara'. The content of The Bhagavad Gita is the conversation between Lord Krishna and Arjuna that took place on the battlefield before the start of the Kurukshetra war. It is the most popular and well known of all the sacred scriptures from ancient India.

Bhishma : One of the most honoured figures of the Indian epic, The Mahabhatata. To the people of India, he is the symbol of mature wisdom.

Brahman : According to Hinduism, Brahman is the unchanging, infinite, immanent and transcendent reality which is the Divine ground of all matter, energy, time, space, being and everything beyond this universe.

Brahmarishi : A sage who has understood the meaning of 'Brahman' or has attained the highest divine knowledge 'Brahmajnana'.

Bhrama Sutra : Hindu religious scripture, attributed to Badarayana in which the teachings of Vedanta are set forth in a systematic and logical order.

Brihadaranyak Upanishad : One of the oldest 'Upanishads', dating to roughly 8th to 5th century B.C. Its name is literally translated as 'Great forest teaching'.

Buddha : Siddhartha Gautama, who came to be known as 'the Buddha' was born a Prince in a place called Lumbini in 560 B.C. Lumbini was originally in northern India, but is now a part of Nepal. Gautama was Siddharta's family name. The word Buddha refers to 'one to whom truth is known'. Siddhartha attained enlightenment at the age of 35. Buddha preached 'The Four Noble Truths' to his disciples, who in turn preached them to the people of their time and this led to the origin of Buddhism, which has grown into one of the greatest religions of the world.

Chanakya : He was also known as 'Kautilya' and 'Vishnugupta'. He was one of the earliest political thinkers lived during the period 350 – 275 B.C. He is the author of two famous books 'Arthasashtra' and 'Neetisashtra', which is also known as 'Chanakya Neeti'. He is believed to be the Chief Minister in the court of the Indian emperor 'Chandragupta Maurya', a contemporary of Alexander.

Chandogya Upanishad : One of the oldest Upanishads, associated with the Samaveda.

Chanakya Neeti : The teachings of 'Chanakya'. This is also known as 'Neetisashtra'.

Chinmayananda : An Indian philosopher and religious teacher who is one of the 20th century's most world-renowned and revered exponents of Vedanta. (1916 – 1993)

Dayananda Saras-wathi : Born in 1930, a monk of the Hindu monastic order and a renouned teacher of Advaita Vedanta.

Deva : A demigod or a minor deity, who is a resident of heaven (according to Hindu mythology).

Dhammapada : Sacred text of the Buddhists. It explains the path of Dharma and consists of 423 verses in Pali language, uttered by the Buddha on some 305 occasions, for the benefit of mankind.

Dharma : Dharma is the path of righteousness and living one's life according to the codes of conduct as prescribed by the Hindu Scriptures.

Garuda : A large mythical bird-like creature that appears both in Hindu and Buddhist mythology.

Garuda purana : One of the 'puranas' which are part of the Hindu body of texts known as 'smriti'. It consists of instructions by Lord 'Vishnu' to his carrier 'Garuda'.

Gautama Buddha : See 'Buddha'.

Gautamananda : He is the president of Sri Ramakrishna Math, Chennai since 1995 and a trustee of the Ramakrishna Math & Mission since 1990. He was ordained into *Sannayas* in 1996. Swamiji speaks and writes on Ramakrishna-Vivekananda philosophy and on Indian culture.

Gitanjali : One of Rabindranath Tagore's most famous works that led to Tagore being the first Asian to be awarded the Nobel Prize for literature. It is a collection of 103 poems. It is known for its lyrical beauty and spiritual poignancy. It was written in 1910 after Tagore lost his father, wife, second daughter and youngest son.

Guna : The quality of nature that binds one's self to the world.

Japa : Meditative repetition of a 'Mantra' or God's name.

J.Krishnamurthy : (Jiddu Krishnamurthy). He was a renowned Indian philosopher and religious teacher. (1895 – 1986). He is regarded as one of the greatest thinkers and religious teachers. He did not subscribe to any school of political, ideological or spiritual thought. His teachings transcend man-made belief systems.

Isavasyopa Upanishad : It is considered as the 'Gem' among all 108 Upanishads. This contains just 18 verses and contains the essence of all knowledge that has been contemplated and experienced by Indian thinkers.

Janaka : Father of 'Sita' in the epic The Ramayana. He was not only a brave king, but also as well-versed in the 'Vedas' as any 'Rishi'.

Jeevan Mukta : The person who is liberated while still living in this world.

J.P. Vaswani : A prolific author and philosopher. He is the spiritual head of Sadhu Vaswani Mission in Pune, India.

Kabir	:	A mystic poet and saint of India (1440 – 1518) whose poems are known for their content of love and devotion to God.
Kahlil Gibran	:	A Lebanese-American mystical poet and philosophical essayist. (1883 – 1931).
Kautilya	:	See 'Chanakya'.
Karma	:	A concept of Hinduism which explains causality through a system where beneficial effects are derived from past beneficial actions and harmful actions from past harmful actions, creating a system of actions and reactions throughout a person's reincarnated lives. According to Buddhism 'karma' is the law of moral causation and is the fundamental doctrine through which Buddha explained the nature of existence in its many ways and forms.
Koushitaki Upanishad	:	An Upanishad associated with the 'Rig Veda'.
Lao – Tzu	:	A philosopher of ancient China, believed to have lived between 600 & 300 B.C.
Leo Tolstoy	:	A Russian essayist and philosopher (1828 – 1910).
Mahabharata	:	The Mahabharata is one of the two major Sanskrit epics on ancient India, the other being 'The Ramayana'. This epic forms an important part of Hindu mythology.
Maitri Upanishad	:	One of the Upanishads that is a branch of Yajur Veda.
Manu Dharma Sastra	:	See 'Manusmriti'.
Manusmriti	:	Also known as 'Manu Dharma Sastra', is a discourse given by 'Manu' to a group of seers. According to Hinduism, Manusmriti records the words of Brahma. 'Manu' is considered as the first law-giver in the history of mankind. Manusmriti contains 2700 verses.
Matsya Purana	:	One of the eighteen puranas in the Hindu scriptures, said to have been communicated to the seventh Manu, Vaivasvata, by Lord Vishnu, in the form of a fish.

Mata Amritananda-mayi : A world renowned Indian saint, popularly called 'Amma'. She is known to bestow her unconditional love on people from all walks of life. She is also known for her humanitarian activities throughout the Globe.

Maya : Illusion.

Mohammed : The founder of the religion of Islam.

Neeti Neri : One of the literary works of 17th century Tamil saint Kumaraguruparar who was a poet of considerable genius, a philosopher of great acumen and a powerful religious organizer.

Nir-guna : Free from the influence of 'Gunas'.

Nirmalananda : Swami Nirmalananda (1863 – 1938) was a monk of the Ramakrishna Order.

Osho : An Indian mystic and spiritual teacher who garnered an international following. He was born on 11 December 1931 in Kuchwada, a small village in the state of Madhya Pradesh, India. He was also known as Bhagwan Shree Rajneesh. He is said to have attained enlightenment (or 'Samadhi') at the age of 21. He passed away on 19 January, 1990. He was one of the most famed as well as the most controversial spiritual leaders of his time.

Padma Purana : One of the eighteen puranas in the Hindu scriptures, containing explanation of Metaphysical knowledge.

Paramahansa Yogananda : (1893 – 1952) An Indian saint who was the principle disciple of Swami Yukteswari Giri. He introduced the soul-awakening techniques of 'Kriya Yoga', a sacred spiritual science originating millenniums ago in India.

Patanjali Maharishi : A Maharishi who is the compiler of 'Yoga Sutra'. He is considered to be the incarnation of Adi Sesha, the infinite cosmic serpent upon whom Lord Vishnu rests.

Padma Purana : One of the eighteen 'puranas' of Hinduism.

Paul Tillich	:	A German-American theologian. (born: 1886; died: 1965).
Pranayama	:	It is the science of breath control. It is one of the five principles of 'Yoga'.
Prasada	:	A gracious gift; usually refers to the gifts of God.
Puranas	:	A group of important Hindu (or jain or Buddhist) religious texts. They are usually written in the form of stories related by one person to another.
Rabindranath Tagore	:	A Nobel-prize winning Indian poet, who was also a social and religious reformer and a philosopher (1861 – 1941).
Rama (Lord Rama)	:	The seventh 'Avatar' of 'Vishnu' in Hinduism.
Ramayana	:	The Ramayana is one of the two major Sanskrit epics on ancient India, the other being 'The Mahabharata'. This epic forms an important part of Hindu mythology.
Rishi	:	A seer to whom the Vedas were 'originally revealed' through states of higher consciousness.
Rig Veda	:	The oldest of the four Vedas. Scholars date the Rig Veda as before 4000 B.C. Many aspects of Vedic science like the practice of Yoga, Meditation, Mantra and Ayurveda are found in the Rig Veda.
S. Radhakrishnan	:	(Sarvepalli Radhakrishnan). He was an Indian philosopher and statesman. He was the first vice-president of India. He was one of India's most influential scholars of comparative religion and philosophy.(1888 – 1975)
Saint Thayumanavar	:	See 'Thayumanavar'.
Saint Valmiki	:	See 'Valmiki'.
Saivism	:	A religious tradition that regards Lord Siva as the highest supreme Self or 'Brahman'.
Sama Veda	:	The second of the four Vedas. Its earliest parts are believed to date from 1000 B.C.
Samakaras	:	They are subtle impressions that are made in the mind whenever we do actions (consciously).

Memories are recent impressions. Human beings are believed to have countless impressions from many pervious births.

Sankhya School : A school of philosophy belonging to ancient India. This is considered to be founded by a philosopher named Kapila. Buddhism is believed to have borrowed many ideas from Sankhya School.

Satya : Truth.

Satya Sai Baba : A spiritual leader and world teacher. He is considered by his devotees as an 'Avatar'. He was born on 23 November, 1926 in a remote village of Puttaparthi, in Andhra Pradesh, India.

Shakti : Personification of divine feminine creative power in Hinduism; also referred to as 'the Great divine Mother'.

Shiva Gita : It is a text of Vedantic 'Saivism' and it forms part of 'Padma purana'. In this, the teacher is Lord Siva and the disciple is Lord Rama.

Sivananda : Swami Sivananda (1887 – 1963) was one of the greatest Indian Yoga masters of the 20th century. The teachings of Swami Sivananada are summarized in six words: Serve, Love, Purify, Mediate, realize.

Sloka : A Sanskrit word used to denote a prayerful verse, written as per certain grammatical rules.

Smriti : Writings containing teachings of the sages, the epics and the puranas.

Sreemad Bhagavatam : One of the important classics of India, describing the life and times of Lord Krishna. It is considered as the Hindu Bible.

Sri Aurobindo : See 'Aurobindo'.

Shukra Neeti : The teachings of Guru 'Shukracharya', who was a Hindu sage. According to Hindu mythology, Shukracharya was the son of 'Vidhata' who was the son of Maharishi Bhrigu. He used to give religious discourses to

'Asuras' (in Hinduism, the Asura are known as a group of power-seeking deities, sometimes referred to as Demons or sinful) to change their evil nature. Though being a Guru of 'Asuras' he was a great devotee of Lord Vishnu.

Subramanya Bharati : (1882 – 1921) A Tamil poet, reformer and freedom fighter. He was an ardent devotee of 'Shakti' and was deeply religious.

Sue Patton Thoele : A psychotherapist and an author of many books.

Swami Chinmayananda : See 'Chinmayananda'.

Swami Dayananda Saraswathi : See 'Dayananda Saraswathi'.

Swami Gautamananda : See 'Gautamananda'.

Swami Nirmalananda : See 'Nirmalananda'.

Swami Sivananda : See 'Sivananda'.

Swami Turiyananda : See 'Turiyananda'.

Swami Vivekananda : See 'Vivekananda'.

Tagore : See 'Rabindranath Tagore'.

Thirukkural : It is the masterpiece of Tamil literature. It was written by Tamil saint poet 'Thiruvalluvar' and is in the form of couplets (two line poems), expounding various aspects of human life. Thirukkural has been translated into most languages, next only to the Bible.

Thiruvalluvar : A celebrated Tamil poet who wrote 'Thirukkural'. His period has been estimated to be between 200 B.C. and 10 B.C. He is considered as one of the great intellectuals that history has ever seen.

Thoreau : An American author, poet and philosopher (1817 – 1862).

Tulasidass : (or 'Tulsidas' 1532 – 1623) was a great philosopher and poet and a devotee of Lord Rama. He is considered to be the reincarnation of Sage Valmiki.

Tukaram : A 17th century Marathi poet. He was an ardent devote of Lord Vittala, an incarnation of Lord Krishna.

Turiyananda : Swami Turiyananda (1863 – 1922) was a monk of the Ramakrishna order and an associate of Swami Vivekananda.

Uddhava Gita : Teachings of Lord Krishna to His friend 'Uddhava'. It is a part of Sreemad Bhagavatam.

Upanishads : Hindu scriptures that contain the core teachings of 'Vedanta'.

Vaishnavite : The followers of 'Vaishnavism' are referred to as Vaishnavites. Vaishnavism is a tradition of Hinduism, distinguished from other schools by its worship of Vishnu or His associated 'Avatars'.

Vallalar : A great Tamil saint (1823 – 1874) of the nineteenth century. He performed many miracles. On the last day of his existence, he left the world without any trace. He is believed to have dissolved his body into 'jhoti' (light).

Valmiki : A celebrated poet who is the author of the epic 'The Ramayana'. He was a highway robber by profession. He came under the spell of Maharishi Naradha and became a 'Brahmarishi'.

Vasana : These are the innate tendencies in Human beings that are responsible for the perceptions, emotions, thoughts and actions. According to Hinduism, Vasanas are brought from previous births. They are the effect of *samakaras.*

Vasishta : A great saint who was the preceptor of Lord Rama and Harischandra. He is considered to be the one who conquered anger and desire.

Vaswani : See 'J.P. Vaswani'.

Vedas : The primary texts of Hinduism. There are four Vedas, viz., the Rig Veda, Sama Veda, Yajur Veda and Atharva Veda. The Rig Veda is considered to be the oldest, and was composed about 1500 B.C.

Vedanta	:	It literally means 'the end of the 'Vedas'; but, it refers to the teachings of the Upanishads and the knowledge of the Ultimate.
Vidhura Neeti	:	These are the moral teachings of Vidhura to his elder brother Dhrithashtra and forms part of 'Udyog Parva' of the great Indian epic 'The Mahabharata'.
Vishnu	:	(Lord Vishnu) The supreme God in the 'Vaishnavite' tradition of Hinduism.
Vishnu Purana	:	One of the eighteen puranas in the Hindu scriptures, pertaining to the Vaishnava branch of Hinduism.
Vivekananda	:	Swami Vivekananda (1863 – 1902) is the chief disciple of the 19th century mystic Sri Ramakrishna (also known as Sri Ramakrishna Paramahamsa). He is the main Indian monk who introduced the concepts of 'Vedanta' and 'Yoga' to Europe and America.
Yajur Veda	:	The third of the four Vedas. It is estimated to have been composed between 1400 & 1000 B.C.
Yajnavalkya Upanishad	:	The Upanishad named after the legendary sage of Vedic India, Yajnavalkya.
Yaksha	:	A broad class of nature-spirits that are found in Hindu, Jain and Buddhist mythology, who are care-takers of hidden natural treasures.
Yoga	:	The Sanskrit word 'Yoga' means 'union'. It is an ancient Indian science that leads to healthy body, peaceful mind, joyous heart and liberated soul.
Yoga Sutra	:	This is the foundational text of 'Yoga' and is believed to had been complied by Patanjali Maharishi during 2nd century, B.C.
Yoga Vasishta	:	It is a work of about 32,000 Sanskrit couplets, traditionally attributed to Valmiki, the author of the great epic The Ramayana. It is a dialogue between sage Vasishta and Lord Rama, during which, Advaita (the doctroine of non-duality) in its pure form is expounded.

Yogi Vemmanna : A 14th century Telugu poet and saint. His poems discuss the subjects of yoga, wisdom and morality.

Yudhishthira : He is the eldest of the five pandava brothers and is one of the principal heroes of the Mahabharata. He possessed virtuous character and is a strict follower of Dharma.

Zen : A school of Buddhism.

Zoroaster : An ancient Iranian prophet and philosopher who is believed to have lived between 1750 and 1500 BC.

Index